This book is to be returned on or before
the last date stamped below

POETRY
OF THE FORTIES

*

INTRODUCED AND EDITED BY
ROBIN SKELTON

PENGUIN BOOKS

Penguin Books Ltd, Harmondsworth, Middlesex, England
Viking Penguin Inc., 40 West 23rd Street, New York, New York 10010, U.S.A.
Penguin Books Australia Ltd, Ringwood, Victoria, Australia
Penguin Books Canada Limited, 2801 John Street, Markham, Ontario, Canada L3R 1B4
Penguin Books (N.Z.) Ltd, 182–190 Wairau Road, Auckland 10, New Zealand

—

First published 1968
Reprinted 1987

—

Copyright © Robin Skelton, 1968
All rights reserved

—

Printed and bound in Great Britain by
Cox & Wyman Ltd, Reading
Typeset in Monotype Baskerville

Contents

'THAT BATTLE-FIT WE LIVED...'

CONTENTS

'THE TRAVELLER HAS REGRETS...'

'OPENING A WAY THROUGH TIME...'

CONTENTS

'NOW THERE IS NOTHING NEW...'

CONTENTS

Acknowledgements

For permission to reprint poems in this anthology, acknowledgement is made to the following:

For DRUMMOND ALLISON: 'The Brass Horse', 'Wade', and 'A Great Unhealthy Friendship', from *The Yellow Night*, to Fortune Press Ltd.

For KENNETH ALLOTT: 'Departure Platform', to the author.

For PATRICK ANDERSON: 'Desert', to the author.

For W. H. AUDEN: 'The Dark Years', from *Collected Shorter Poems, 1927–1957*, to Faber and Faber Ltd.

For GEORGE BARKER: 'Elegy I', 'To My Mother', 'News of the World III', and 'Channel Crossing', from *Collected Poems 1930–55*, to Faber and Faber Ltd.

For JOHN BAYLISS: 'The Wreck', and 'Seven Dreams', to the author.

For WILLIAM BELL: 'On a Dying Boy', and 'The Chief Stoker's Song', from *Mountains Beneath the Horizon*, 1950, to Faber and Faber Ltd.

For DEMETRIOS CAPETANAKIS: 'Lazarus', 'Abel', and 'Detective Story', to John Lehmann.

For LEONARD CLARK: 'Good Friday', and 'Encounter', to the author.

For ALEX COMFORT: 'Seventh Elegy' from *Elegies*, 1944, and an extract from 'The Sleeping Princess', from *And All But He Departed*, 1951, to Routledge and Kegan Paul Ltd.

For DORIAN COOKE: 'A Soldier, Dying of Wounds', and 'Poem on Returning Home', to the author.

For R. N. CURREY: 'Burial Flags, Sind', to the author.

For PAUL DEHN: 'Spring Song, 1948', and 'Armistice', from *The Fern on the Rock*, to the author and Hamish Hamilton Ltd.

For PATRIC DICKINSON: 'Ultima Thule', 'War', 'A Warning to Politicians', and 'Lust', to the author.

For KEITH DOUGLAS: 'Simplify Me When I'm Dead', 'Behaviour of Fish in an Egyptian Tea Garden', 'Cairo Jag', and 'On a Return from Egypt', from *Collected Poems*, to Faber and Faber Ltd.

For LAWRENCE DURRELL: 'This Unimportant Morning', and 'Phileremo', from *Collected Poems*, to Faber and Faber Ltd.

For D. J. ENRIGHT: 'By the Middle Sea', from *The Laughing Hyena*, to Routledge and Kegan Paul Ltd.

For ROBIN FEDDEN: 'An Undistinguished Coast', to the author.

For G. S. FRASER: 'The Traveller Has Regrets', and 'Egypt', to the author.

For ERNEST FROST: 'Italy', to the author. (This poem was first published in *Four in Hand . . . an Excursion*, Three Arts Club, Naples, 1945.)

For ROY FULLER: 'The Middle of a War', 'During a Bombardment by V-Weapons', 'The Giraffes', 'The Civilization', 'Virtue', and 'The Photographs', from *Collected Poems 1936–61*, to André Deutsch Ltd.

For ROLAND GANT: 'The Wedding', to the author.

For WREY GARDINER: 'Wild Olive', to the author.

For DAVID GASCOYNE: 'A Wartime Dawn', 'Ecce Homo', and 'A Vagrant', from *Collected Poems*, 1965, to Oxford University Press Ltd.

For W. S. GRAHAM: 'To My Father', 'Since All My Steps Taken', 'Listen. Put on Morning', and 'Men Sign the Sea', all from *The White Threshold*, 1949, to Faber and Faber Ltd.

For BERNARD GUTTERIDGE: 'Tananarive', to the author.

For MICHAEL HAMBURGER: 'From the Notebook of a European Tramp XI', to the author.

For JOHN HEATH-STUBBS: 'Maria Aegyptiaca', 'The Divided Ways', and 'Drowned Man', from *Selected Poems*, 1965, to the author and Oxford University Press Ltd.

For ALEXANDER HENDERSON: 'Sea of Marmora', from *The Tunnelled Fire*, to the author and Secker and Warburg Ltd.

For J. F. HENDRY: 'London Before Invasion 1940', from *The Bombed Happiness*, 1942, to Routledge and Kegan Paul Ltd.

For SEAN JENNET: 'Cycle: VI', and 'Hereafter', from *The Cloth of Flesh*, to Faber and Faber Ltd.

For SIDNEY KEYES: 'William Wordsworth', 'War Poet', 'Europe's Prisoners', 'Troll Kings', and 'Sour Land', from *Collected Poems*, 1945, to Routledge and Kegan Paul Ltd.

For FRANCIS KING: 'The Patient', to the author; for 'Seance' and 'The Carcase', from *Rod of Incantation*, to Longmans Green and Co. Ltd.

For JAMES KIRKUP: 'Elegy for a Dead God', to the author.

For CHRISTOPHER LEE: 'Midsummer 1942' and 'Trahison des Clercs' (the latter quoted in the introduction to this book), from *Under the Sun*, 1948, to the author and The Bodley Head Ltd.

For LAURIE LEE: 'Day of These Days', 'April Rise', and 'Bird', from *The Bloom of Candles*, John Lehmann Ltd, 1947, to the author and Laurence Pollinger Ltd.

For PATRICK LEIGH FERMOR: 'Greek Archipelagoes', to the author and John Murray Ltd.

For ALUN LEWIS: 'Corfe Castle', and 'All Day it has Rained', from *Raiders Dawn*, 1942, and 'Goodbye', 'Bivouac', 'The Mahratta Ghats', and 'The Jungle', from *Ha! Ha! Among the Trumpets*, 1945, to George Allen and Unwin Ltd.

For C. DAY LEWIS: 'Watching Post', from *Collected Poems 1954*, and 'Where are the War Poets?' (the latter quoted in the introduction to this book), to Jonathan Cape Ltd.

For ROBERT LIDDELL: 'Dead Sea Plage', and 'On a War Poet' (the latter quoted in the introduction to this book), to the author.

For EMANUEL LITVINOFF: 'African Village', to the author.

For LOUIS MACNEICE: 'Refugees', from *Collected Poems*, to Faber and Faber Ltd.

For NORMAN MCCAIG: 'The dizzy summer calf', from *Far Cry*, 1943, to Routledge and Kegan Paul Ltd.

For NEIL MCCALLUM: 'Stand-To', to the author and Curtis Brown Ltd.

For J. C. MOLLISON: 'Mokomeh Ghat', to the author.

For JAMES MONAHAN: 'The Album', to the author.

For NICHOLAS MOORE: 'Ideas of Disorder at Torquay', from *The Cabaret, the Dancer, the Gentlemen*, 1942, to Fortune Press Ltd.

For NORMAN NICHOLSON: 'Cockley Moor', and 'Belshazzar', from *Five Rivers*, and 'Rock Face', and 'Early March', from *Rock Face*, to Faber and Faber Ltd.

For JULIAN ORDE: 'The Changing Wind', to the author.

For MERVYN PEAKE: 'Is There No Love Can Link Us?', and 'London 1941', from *Shapes and Sounds*, 1941, to the author and Chatto and Windus Ltd.

For F. T. PRINCE: 'Soldiers Bathing', from *The Doors of Stone, Poems 1938–62*, 1963, to the author and Rupert Hart-Davis Ltd.

For KATHLEEN RAINE: 'The Moment', 'The End of Love', 'Envoi', 'Air', and 'Woman to Lover', all from *Collected Poems*, 1956, to the author and Hamish Hamilton Ltd.

For HENRY REED: 'Lessons of the War', and 'The Wall', from *A Map of Verona*, 1946, to Jonathan Cape Ltd.

For ANNE RIDLER: 'Kirkwall 1942', from *The Nine Bright Shiners*, to Faber and Faber Ltd.

For IVOR ROBERTS-JONES: 'Battalion H.Q., Burma', to the author.

For W. R. RODGERS: 'Express', and 'Stormy Day', from *Awake! and other poems*, 1941, and 'Christ Walking on the Water',

ACKNOWLEDGEMENTS

from *Europa and the Bull*, 1952, to Secker & Warburg Ltd.

For ALAN ROOK: 'Dunkirk Pier', from *Soldiers, This Solitude*, 1942, to Routledge and Kegan Paul Ltd.

For ALAN ROSS: 'Cricket at Brighton', and 'Survivors', from *Poems 1942–67*, to Eyre and Spottiswoode (Publishers) Ltd.

For VERNON SCANNELL: 'Aftermath', from *Graves and Resurrections*, 1948, to Fortune Press Ltd.

For FRANCIS SCARFE: 'Tyne Dock', to the author.

For BERNARD SPENCER: 'On a Carved Axlepiece', 'On the Road', 'Greek Excavations', and 'Out of Sleep', from *Collected Poems*, 1965, to Alan Ross Ltd.

For RICHARD SPENDER: 'Tunisian Patrol', from *Collected Poems of Richard Spender*, to Sidgwick and Jackson Ltd, and the author's representatives.

For STEPHEN SPENDER: 'June 1940', from *Collected Poems*, 1955, to Faber and Faber Ltd.

For HAL SUMMERS: 'The Seed', to the author.

For JULIAN SYMONS: 'Pub', and 'The Clock', from *The Second Man*, 1943, and 'Homage to Our Leaders' (the latter quoted in the introduction to this book), to Routledge and Kegan Paul Ltd.

For R. S. THOMAS: 'A Peasant', and 'Out of the Hills', from *Song at the Year's Turning*, 1955, to Rupert Hart-Davis Ltd, and the author.

For DYLAN THOMAS: 'Fern Hill', 'Poem in October', 'A Refusal to Mourn', and 'A Winter's Tale', to J. M. Dent and Sons Ltd, and the Trustees of the Copyrights of the late Dylan Thomas.

For FRANK THOMPSON: 'London 1940', 'Day's Journey', and 'De Amicitia', from *There is a Spirit in Europe*, Gollancz, 1947, to Mr E. P. Thompson.

For TERENCE TILLER: 'Beggar', and 'Spring Letter', from *Unarm, Eros*, 1947, 'Egyptian Dancer', from *The Inward Animal*, 1943, and 'Nocturnal III', from *Poems*, 1941, to the author and the Hogarth Press Ltd.

For RUTHVEN TODD: 'Personal History', from *Until Now*, to Fortune Press Ltd.

For HENRY TREECE: 'Three Pleas', and 'Relics', from *The Black Seasons*, to Faber and Faber Ltd.

For JAMES WALKER: 'Balloon Barrage', and 'Lying Awake', from *Against the Sun*, Fortune Press, 1946, to the author.

For VERNON WATKINS: 'Griefs of the Sea', from *The Ballad of the Mari Lwyd*, and 'The Feather', and 'The Healing of the Leper', from *The Lady With the Unicorn*, to Faber and Faber Ltd.

For PAUL WIDDOWS: 'Perspective', to the author.

Introduction

The forties in England began with war and ended with social revolution. The social structure which provided the poets of the thirties with their themes of criticism and anxiety was altered, first by violence and then by statute. It was a period of crisis and transition, and the poetry of the decade is filled with themes of uncertainty and romance. Much of this work does not survive its times; it described and satisfied psychological needs peculiar to an environment that no longer exists, and, as a consequence, many of the poets found notable by those years now appear to be dismal failures.

This has made the compilation of this anthology extremely difficult, for there are two ways of tackling such a problem. The first is to present the forties' own version of its poetry by selecting the works fashionable at the time and by representing most fully those 'schools' and 'movements' which were most in the public eye. The second method is to choose those poems which now appear to be most successful, and which may speak the more efficiently to our own time because they avoided the obsessions of their own. I have chosen, in the main, to follow the latter plan, while doing my best not to misrepresent the historical situation. Thus, I have omitted work by many poets whose names might be expected to appear on my table of contents, and I have included work by several whose names were then, and still are, unfamiliar to most of us.

I have made a number of perhaps arbitrary decisions about the poets to be included. First, I decided that I should not include the work of any poet whose reputation was fully established before 1940 unless that poet made such a considerable contribution to the decade that he could not justly be ignored. Once I had made this decision I discovered that the number of exceptions to my rule had to be somewhat large. Kenneth Rexroth in his anthology *New British Poets* (1949) stated, 'If Auden dominated the recent past, Dylan Thomas dominates the present,' and other critics have identified the three dominant figures of the decade as Dylan Thomas, David Gascoyne, and George Barker. It was in the forties that the 'new generation of poets' which C. Day Lewis described as emerging in the middle thirties really came into their own, and no forties anthology could decently exclude the work of Bernard Spencer, Lawrence Durrell, Roy Fuller, Terence Tiller, Kathleen Raine, and many others already well established before the decade began. In any case several of these writers did not produce their first collections until the forties, and so they were covered by my further decision to include work by any poet whose first book appeared within the decade, regardless of his or her age.

This second decision was forced upon me by the realization that the war caused several people to emerge as poets who had not been known for their poetry previously. Nevertheless, once I started to check the birth dates of my candidates for inclusion I discovered that, while a 'forties generation' is not as easily identifiable as a 'thirties generation', almost all the writers I thought admissible were born between 1912 and 1922, and thus were between the ages of 18 and 28 when the decade began.

The presence of the younger thirties poets as key figures of the forties period may lead one to expect a certain continuity of approach from one decade to the other. This is, in part, the case; the romanticism of the forties owes much to that of the later thirties. Nevertheless, while many of the forties poets were enthusiastic about

the earlier work of Thomas, Gascoyne, Barker and their
close contemporaries, a large number were very much
opposed to the poetry of Auden and the 'New Country'
school of writers which appeared in the early thirties.

This opposition was partly a confessedly 'romantic'
rebellion against the supposedly 'classical' approach of
Auden and the magazine *New Verse*. It was also, however,
the result of a loss of faith. Just as the thirties poets
lamented the loss of a leader when T. S. Eliot turned to
Anglo-Catholicism and hob-nobbed with the Fascists in
Portugal, so the forties poets saw Auden's departure for
America as a betrayal. Christopher Lee called his poem
on the subject *Trahison des Clercs*.

> One sailed for New York: a second followed;
> one at that moment broke his heart for a woman,
> showing the pieces to strangers in cafés,
> making of the world's calamity
> a mirror of his own sensitiveness;
> the fourth held his tongue. These the men
> – flown, flying, broken or checked pen –
> the poets we took for leaders, who should speak
> for those who could not, make
> bridges and barricades for all of us.
> It is their own concern: honest perhaps,
> perhaps wise – except for him who sees
> wherever he looks his own quivering face –
> time and their work will weigh their choice.
> But what of us
> remaining, so perplexed:
> shall we still honour poets of the people, look
> for wisdom in their words, or vexed
> watch down the wind these swift migrating birds?

Cyril Connolly's comment in the second issue of *Horizon*
(February 1940) was less passionate.

The flight of Auden and Isherwood to a land richer in incident and opportunity is also a symptom of the failure of social realism as an aesthetic doctrine ... We believe that a reaction away from social realism is as necessary and salutary as was, a generation ago, the reaction from the Ivory Tower.

The elder poets of the thirties did not, of course, abandon their concern for the predicament of England in the way Lee and Connolly appear to suggest, and I have chosen to give Auden, Day Lewis, MacNeice and Spender the role of Prologue in this anthology, for their comments of 1940 indicate brilliantly the mood of the times, and show that, despite all their desires to the contrary, many of the forties romantics derived a good deal of their approach from the approaches of their elders.

There was, however, a change, though it was brought about more by the alteration of living conditions than by the adoption of a particular literary programme. The old tools required adjusting, but there was no need to throw them away.

It is hard to describe the effect of the outbreak of war upon England. Almost every aspect of living was affected. Black-out regulations, air-raid warnings, and the rationing of food, petrol and clothing altered everybody's way of life. The countryside was dotted with army camps, searchlight and anti-aircraft batteries, and newly created airfields. The beaches were soon cluttered with pill-boxes, barbed wire entanglements, and concrete defence works. The sky and the sea grew ominous, and strangers became suspect.

These were unpleasant, though often stimulating, changes. Other innovations were less harmful. Unemployment ended. Rationing brought with it a concern for nutrition that led to better health for all the children and most of the adults. Social barriers crumbled in the common experience of air-raids, and patriotic messages gave something of a feeling of unity and purpose to what Auden had called 'This England of ours where nobody is well'.

In the face of this the poets appeared, initially, to be at a loss. The newspapers asked 'Where are the War Poets?' and mourned the absence of latter-day Grenfells, Sorleys, and Brookes. The poets replied sourly. C. Day Lewis wrote:

Where are the War Poets?

They who in folly or mere greed
Enslaved religion, markets, laws,
Borrow our language now and bid
Us to speak up in freedom's cause.

It is the logic of our times,
No subject for immortal verse –
That we who lived by honest dreams
Defend the bad against the worse.

War Poets did, of course, emerge, but most of those who gave the newspapers what they wanted are now forgotten. Robert Liddell was derisive on the subject.

On a War Poet

How fit that you should write about the War
And tell us what they fought each other for –
An empty skull upon a village green
Did this for Peterkin and Wilhelmine.

The poets were, however, involved in the war, for everybody was involved. They were not, however, enthusiastic about it. Ronald Blythe stated the situation very well when he wrote in his introduction to his anthology of wartime writing, *Components of the Scene* (Penguin Books, 1966):

The great thing was not to pretend, or proffer solutions, or to be histrionic. Each poet spoke as wholly and truthfully as he could from out of the one inviolable spot of an otherwise violated order, his own identity. This he found more threatened by the inanities of the barracks, wartime bureaucrats and those countless inroads upon the dignity of the person which a national emergency prescribes, than by the terrible etiquette of the battlefield.

The theme of lost or threatened identity gave rise to much poetry of the time. The image of the drowned man appeared frequently; there were at least half a dozen poems on the suicide, by drowning, of the American poet Hart Crane in 1932, and the favourite myths of the period were those concerning the dead or dying god of the fertility rituals described in Frazer's *The Golden Bough* and exploited in the poetry of T. S. Eliot.

These were somewhat oblique reactions. Some were more direct. Julian Symons's poem of 1943 is an indication of the attitude of many writers in the war years.

Homage to Our Leaders

These larger-than-life comic characters,
Churchill the moonface moocow chewing
A permanent cigar, Roosevelt the gigantic
False Liberal mask with syrup smile,
Medicine-man Stalin like Aunt Sally at a fair,
All snapping like canvas in the wind . . .

Our world, our time, our murder
Evolved these monsters: who like the allosaurus
Should be remembered as a stupidity
We have outgrown. Now they sprawl across
Hoardings, papers, radios, these simple shapeless demons.
Friend, lock your door at night: watch neighbour and wife,
See that your eyes are hidden behind dark glasses,
Remember that you live by permission of the police.

Though flag-waving patriotism did not appeal to the poets of the forties, and they were distrustful of authority, the threat of invasion caused them to look again at their national inheritance, and to attempt to grapple with that strange love of one's own place which alone gives meaning to the generalized rhetoric of the politicians. They found, as Edward Thomas had found in 1914, that the threat of destruction made them aware of the sharpness of their affections, and turned to themes of natural beauty and to regionalism.

Naturally, this trend was most obvious in the work of poets who lived in areas with strong local identities. The Welsh produced the magazine *Wales*, and gave us the exuberant lyricism of Dylan Thomas and Vernon Watkins as well as the harshly affectionate studies of R. S. Thomas and Roland Mathias. Scotland provided *Poetry Scotland* and the poems of George Bruce, W. S. Graham, Norman McCaig, and Neil McCallum. Norman Nicholson wrote of his native Cumberland, and others found excitement in the landscapes of Cornwall and Northern Ireland.

This new regionalism was, in some ways, a reaction against the growing literary internationalism of the later thirties, but it did not supersede it. Indeed, when John Lehmann began his 'more or less monthly' periodical, *Penguin New Writing*, in 1940, he emphasized the internationalism of his approach, and in the May 1941 issue stated:

We still believe that an important part of our job is to keep alive the awareness of a great modern literature in Europe which has common roots with our own, and will one day rise again when the darkness and destructive influences of the moment have passed.

Cyril Connolly took a similar viewpoint when he began *Horizon* in 1940, and the files of *Poetry Quarterly* and *Poetry (London)* are crammed with translations and foreign contributions. As the decade progressed and the number of refugees and foreign 'free' governments in London swelled, anthologies of European writing became fashionable. Occupied France received the tribute of Nancy Cunard's anthology *Poems for France* (1944), and many French, German, and Italian poems were translated into English for the first time. Moreover, some foreign visitors took to writing in English, the most astonishing of these being Demetrios Capetanakis whose first poem in English, *Detective Story*, I have included in this anthology.

The internationalism of the forties was not caused only by the influx of foreigners and the enthusiasms of the magazine editors, however. As the war dragged on, countless Englishmen found themselves in strange places and felt compelled to explore poetically new landscapes and new societies. The most important group of exiles gathered in Alexandria and produced the quarterly *Personal Landscape* which included work by Lawrence Durrell, Bernard Spencer, Robin Fedden (the three editors), Terence Tiller, Robert Liddell, Keith Douglas, Olivia Manning, Hugh Gordon Porteus and translations of work by Elie Papadimitriou, George Seferis, Cavafy, and Rilke, among others. The anthology *Personal Landscape* appeared in 1945, and, with other anthologies, was largely responsible for the Mediterranean orientation of many English poets of the following generation. No one, certainly, could avoid noticing the number of poets stimulated by their service abroad. John Waller and Erik de Mauny produced their *Middle East Anthology* in 1946. *Poems from the Desert* appeared in 1944 and *Poems from Italy* in 1945. R. N. Currey, farther afield, published his *Poems from India* in 1945, and other poets wrote of Africa, and the Balkans. Unfortunately the poets' concern to report the oddities of foreign parts resulted frequently in the production of verse journalism, and in the weakening of emotional intensity. The reader was to be astonished by anthropology and geography rather than by a new insight into the human predicament. On the other hand, this writing brought much new imagery into the word-hoard of English poetry, and weakened the British tendency towards insularity. The post-war period and the early fifties were to find British poets living and working in most countries of the world for the first time in our history.

Many of the contributors to the overseas anthologies and the many little magazines that appeared during the war never achieved anything but amateurish near-poems, and it seems that when the war was over a good many of them never wrote again. The stimulus of the war, and the so-called 'Poetry Boom', indeed, resulted in the publication of vast quantities of third-rate material. Amateur poetry most usually runs to sentimentality, looseness of form, and pretentious rhetoric, but, in ordinary circumstances, this poetry receives very limited publication and attention. Unfortunately, during the greater part of the decade, the magazines and publishing houses appeared convinced of the existence of a 'new romanticism' which made the acceptance of pretentious and sentimental attitudinizing extremely easy. One of the leaders of this movement was Henry Treece, who founded the 'New Apocalypse' school. He attempted to sum up the nature of the movement in *How I See Apocalypse*, a collection of essays, articles and autobiographical pieces which he published in 1946. In his foreword he wrote:

In my definition, the writer who senses the chaos, the turbulence, the laughter and the tears, the order and the peace of the world in its entirety, is an Apocalyptic writer. His utterances will be prophetic, for he is observing things which less sensitive men have not yet come to notice; and as his words are prophetic, they will tend to be incantatory, and so musical. At times, even, that music may take control, and lead the writer from recording his vision almost to creating another vision. So, momentarily, he will kiss the edge of God's robe.

In an essay *Growing up in Wartime*, he pointed out that the Spanish Civil War, because participating in it was a matter of free individual choice, became 'a symbol of free action, and a stimulus to free thought'. He went on to say:

> But in 1939 the present war had all the terror and the inevitability of cancer; the nightmare had to proceed, however much the patient screamed, protested his innocence, his frightened inability to bear the pain.

This experience of horror, of shock, led him towards greater simplicity of expression and towards a fundamentally religious outlook. It also, however, led him towards rebellion; in *Considerations on Revolt* he expressed sympathy for Herbert Read's version of Anarchism and said:

> I would revolt against the central government that we know and would elevate the local government that so few of us are allowed to respect. I would revolt against the big, industrial city, built and nurtured by the big, industrial magnates. I would revolt against the industrial syndicate, that mad octopus which crushes the life from the men who keep it alive.

This anarchist and romantic rebellion leads him to plead for the emergence of 'a rich and fertile wholeness, a new romanticism, a broader Humanism', and, in other essays, to express opposition to the imagist viewpoint, the 'objective' writing of the poets in *New Verse*, and to indicate the importance of J. F. Hendry's view that

> the poet shall discover and reveal to the world, by reasoning as well as by intuition, by story as well as by image, those fundamental, organic myths which underlie all human endeavour and aspiration, and from the recognition of whose universal application will come a reintegration of the personality with society.

Hendry's and Treece's emphasis upon myth was accepted by many. Poetry became filled with archetypal references and dream imagery. Eliot was now the accepted elder, rather than Auden, and though his doctrine of the 'objective correlative' was unpopular, *The Waste Land* and the *Four Quartets* were highly praised. Many poets attempted an Eliot-like philosophical symbolism. Perhaps the most widely admired poem of this kind was Sidney Keyes's *The Wilderness*, but less derivative though still pretentious poems by others were also given high praise.

John Heath-Stubbs, writing in *Poetry Quarterly* in 1950, said, cuttingly:

From the mass of critical verbiage with which the 'Apocalyptics' sought to define their position it is no more possible, nine years later, for the wit of man to recover a coherent meaning than to reconstruct the song of the Sirens. (But malice may prompt one to return, with quiet amusement, to such passages as that in which Mr Robert Melville instituted a comparison between a poem of Mr Treece and El Greco's *Agony in the Garden*, or where Mr Fraser affirmed that he found Mr Nicholas Moore's mind more interesting than that of Blake.) But one may suspect that, in the end, it all boiled down to this: a general discontent with the social-objective way of writing which prevailed in the thirties, *plus* some rather vague ideas about the importance of 'mythical' imagery. Into this framework were fitted the rhetoric of Mr Hendry, the naïve romanticism of Mr Treece, and the marginal comments of Mr Fraser and Mr Moore (two somewhat tender-minded intellectuals with a taste for the easier forms of English versification) ...

Heath-Stubbs goes on in this essay on Vernon Watkins to suggest that Mr Watkins works 'in the tradition of Yeats rather than in that of Mr Eliot', and Yeats as well as Eliot was a father-figure to many of these romantics.

The doctrines of a period do not necessarily produce its best poetry, and much of the calculated romanticism published in the later forties is hard to take. Nevertheless, once one decides to ignore the judgements of the fashionable commentators, one soon discovers that the best work of the forties is formidably good.

The so-called 'social objectivity' of the early thirties startled by its use of concrete everyday imagery, but often failed because of its wilful pedagogy. The forties work of such poets as Norman Nicholson, R. S. Thomas, and Alun Lewis is just as firmly based upon sensual immediacy and the concrete, but less vitiated by the imposition of theory upon experience. The mountains and landscapes of Auden are allegorical, and serve as fictive environments for the intellectual quandary; the landscape tends to derive from the concept. Alun Lewis's jungle and Norman Nicholson's Cumberland exist as truths of experience, and their actuality gives rise to speculation and philosophy. Even in such a pedagogical poem as Henry Reed's *Lessons of the War*, the allegorical intention appears to spring from the facts, and not vice-versa. When we turn from these poets to those more obviously concerned with myth, we discover that whereas many thirties poets used archetypal symbolism in the service of allegory, the forties poets assumed that the archetypal dream or vision had validity in itself and presented questions which could not be neatly summarized or given fable-like clarity. One has only to contrast the conclusion of John Bayliss's *Seven Dreams* with that of Auden's *The Lesson* to see the difference. Bayliss's poem ends enigmatically:

> And the last door was without a key
> but it lay open to the touch of fingers,
> showing the choir of a church,
> but he found no singers;
> and here lay the fruit like wax
> offerings to the red moon,
> and he saw the four horsemen

engraved on a grey tomb;
and, glowing in stained glass,
the several peacocks stood
admiring themselves in swan's blood,
and he saw the moth dying
in the fading tree, and the black knight beneath
awaiting its last breath;
then a black bat flying disturbed him
and he thought with dismay of the eighth dream
seeing the lake through the small doorway. . . .

Auden's poem contains only three dreams, and concludes:

I woke. You were not there. But as I dressed
Anxiety turned to shame, feeling all three
Intended one rebuke. For had not each
In its own way tried to teach
My will to love you that it cannot be,
As I think, of such consequence to want
What anyone is given, if they want?

Both of these poems are of the forties. Bayliss's first appeared in a book in 1943 and Auden's in 1944. The approach to the dream symbolism is, however, totally different. Bayliss's conclusion suggests many possibilities; Auden limits the possible interpretations of his experience. It is true that the romantics of the forties, while enriching the symbolic potential of their poetry, opened the door to vagueness and melodrama; it is equally true, however, that the intellectual precision of the Auden generation opened the door to doctrinaire pedantry and superficial ingenuity.

The myth-makers of the forties contrast with the poets of the thirties also in their use of history. The 'New Countrymen' used historical references as pedagogical footnotes. The 'New Romantics' attempted to re-create the past rather than use it as an illustration of the present. Thus Sidney Keyes's portrait of Wordsworth is a tribute and celebration whereas Auden's tribute to Yeats is an object lesson. F. T. Prince in *Soldiers Bathing* is less concerned to prove a point than to present the dynamic complexity of any human experience when it is seen in historical depth, and in this he is typical of the forties rather than the thirties in which his first poems appeared. It is Eliot's view of history that operates now, and not the view of Marx and Engels. The great limitation of the 'New Countrymen' was summed up by Dylan Thomas when he called the poetry of Auden 'a hygiene . . . a sanitary science'. The rank odours of love and labour were lost in the stronger odour of lysol. The individual sensibility became a matter of the intelligence, not the senses. The forties poets, sensually assaulted by the new physicalities of wartime and exile, could not remain merely recorders and observers. They rediscovered the body, and sensuality returned to British poetry.

This new sensuality and passion was often undisciplined, of course. Only a few realized that an outcry is not necessarily an insight, and that emotional intensity may outlaw intellectual tension. The poem composed entirely of potent symbols may strike the unconverted as irrational gobbledygook, and the reverent celebrator of the senses may look like a mere sensationalist. Romanticism, however, believes with Blake that 'the road of excess leads to the palace of wisdom', and therefore is always in danger of causing embarrassment. Once the total sensibility is involved, total failure becomes a possibility and total success even more difficult of achievement.

It was the vice and virtue of the 'New Romantics' that they set no limit to their ambitions, and, predictably, it is their smaller poems that are most successful. Dylan Thomas and George Barker could, from time to time, achieve tragic grandeur and prophetic intensity, but the latter fails as often as he succeeds. Kathleen Raine's superb economy of language gave conviction to her mysticism, but Henry Treece and J. F. Hendry approached the ludicrous in their attempt to put the poet back into the sacred priesthood. It was Edith Sitwell who illustrated most dramatically the nature of the New Romantics' pretensions when, at the death of Dylan Thomas, she called him and his work 'holy'. This view may be somewhat extreme, but it indicates graphically the way in which many poets of the forties rejected the view that the poet should be a social commentator, school master, mass observer or lay psychiatrist, and wished him to take on, if not a prophetic mantle, at least a sprig of the divine laurel.

By no means all the poets of the period can be classed as romantics of this dionysiac kind, as the poems in this anthology clearly reveal. Nevertheless, when the poets and critics of the fifties looked back with distaste at the previous decade it was its romanticism that upset them. Much that they found objectionable, however, was the product of the post-war period when the 'Poetry Boom' ended and the confusion of peacetime silenced more poets than it aroused. Moreover, the hindsight of the middle fifties and the sixties revealed that many poets of the forties had not continued in their profession. Francis King, Muriel Spark, and Julian Symons had become novelists. G. S. Fraser had become a critic. Many others had simply fallen silent. Illogically, we tend to assume that the work of a poet whose mortal life continues while his poetry does not is necessarily less important than that of the young poet whose death ended his poetry while he was still in his twenties.

The last years of the forties were, however, difficult for poetry. The publishers lost their enthusiasm for it, and the new magazines had short lives, while the established ones began to peter out. The early fifties saw the death of *Poetry Quarterly*, *Poetry (London)*, *Horizon* and *Penguin New Writing*. In 1951 the Festival of Britain Poetry Competition was a pathetic failure. Enthusiasts attempted to remedy the situation by bringing poetry to the people in pamphlet form. *Key Poets* (1950) edited by Jack Lindsay never ran into a second series. My own *Acadine Poets* (1950–51) lasted less than eighteen months. The Hand and Flower Press series of *Poems in Pamphlet* survived longer, but its productions were unexciting. It was not until the Poetry Book Society was formed, and the P.E.N. sponsored an annual poetry anthology, and the Fantasy Press, Oxford, commenced its influential series of pamphlets devoted to the young that British poetry began to struggle back to health.

The new young poets of the fifties were not romantics. They owed much to the work of Empson, Auden and the 'New Countrymen'. They emphasized the virtues of irony, and thus the forties began to look, as the war had begun to look, like an interim period of delusion and hallucination. Even those young poets whose earliest work had been published during the forties and had been affected by the tastes of the time, now adopted more rigorous and ironic manners, and the new brood of reviewers paid little attention to the work of writers established by the previous decade.

Was the forties period an interlude, however? Was it a passing sickness, a sudden compulsive descent into nightmare? Some men of the fifties believed it to be so, but now, in the sixties, there is some doubt. The *Collected Poems* of Roy Fuller, David Gascoyne, George Barker, Lawrence Durrell, Bernard Spencer, Keith Douglas, Kathleen Raine, and Dylan Thomas are now upon our shelves and cannot be summarily dismissed. Two American romantics of the forties, Theodore Roethke and

Robert Lowell, are now generally appreciated and even imitated. Moreover several of the younger poets of our day now seem to be closer in attitude to the romantic personalism of 1940–45 than to the social objectivism of 1930–35. It is, perhaps, the right moment to re-examine the work of that war-torn decade of social change and psychological uncertainty which temporarily shifted the direction of British poetry, and consider what it has to teach us. It may be, after all, that it was not the forties but the thirties that digressed from the main road. It is a viewpoint worth considering.

ROBIN SKELTON

May 1968
The University of Victoria,
British Columbia

A Note on the Texts Used

I have attempted to indicate the placing of each poem in the decade by dating each of them. The letter 'p' before a date means that the poem was first printed in an anthology or periodical of that year. The letter 'c' means that the poem was published in a collection of work by the poet concerned at that time. Dates without the prefix 'p' or 'c' are those given by the poet himself. I have chosen, however, to add 'p' or 'c' details in most cases, as many poems were first published long after they were written. I have been unable to track down the first printing dates of all the poems, though I would have liked to do so. Thus my dating must be regarded as only an approximate guide, and I hope that interested readers will amend their own copies of the anthology if and when they come across more accurate information.

Many poets revise their work considerably after its first appearance. The texts printed here are those of the dates given, and not those of a later period, with only a few exceptions. The first of these is W. H. Auden's 'The Dark Years'. This poem was first published on 7 December 1940 in *The Nation*. It was then published under the title 'Epilogue' in *New Year Letter* (1941). When it appeared in the *Collected Poetry* (1945) it was called 'Autumn 1940'. The title 'The Dark Years' was first used on its appearance in *Collected Shorter Poems 1927–1957* (1967). I have been obliged to use this latest text, which only differs very slightly indeed, however, from the first version, the differences being mainly in small clarifications of punctuation and minor stylistic improvements.

Other exceptions are the two poems by Alan Ross.

These are presented in the form in which they appear in Mr Ross's *Poems 1942-67* (1967). Mr Ross objected to my original choice of two poems ('Antiques' and 'Islanders') which he has discarded from the canon of his work, and I was happy to be able to choose others which seemed to me almost equally suitable. I was, unfortunately, unable to agree with Patric Dickinson that he should be represented by work from his second collection, *Stone in the Midst* (1948) as well as from his first book, *Theseus and the Minotaur* (1946), and am grateful to him for allowing me to present a perhaps one-sided view of his work.

The following poets have also asked me to include later revised versions of their poems rather than the versions first printed: Paul Dehn, Michael Hamburger, F. T. Prince and Francis Scarfe.

In compiling this anthology I have attempted to present what amounts to a critical essay on the poetry of the times. In so doing I am aware that, by seizing upon poems representative of current themes and obssessions, I may from time to time have done less than justice to the poets concerned. This is inevitable in a 'documentary anthology' of this nature, perhaps, and especially in one which attempts to gather together the work of over eighty poets. Less than justice has certainly been done to many poets who began their poetic careers in the later years of the decade, for they have been represented only by early work. I have, however, done my best to avoid resurrecting poems which are grossly uncharacteristic of their authors, and, for this reason, have not included poems by such poets of the fifties as Philip Larkin, John Wain, Kingsley Amis, and Christopher Middleton, who made their first appearance in periodicals at the end of the period, regarding them as belonging to a different generation.

In the preparation of this work I have been greatly

assisted by a number of people. I must first of all express my thanks to the Manchester City Reference Library where I was able to unearth much material, and to the University of Victoria Library whose collection of twentieth century poetry is impressively large. I am also much in the debt of Mrs Jean Van Cuylenburg and Mrs Gracia Seal for their devoted labours upon the typescript. Others who have drawn my attention to work I might otherwise have missed, or who have assisted me with the loan or gift of periodicals and books, are Tony Connor, J. D. Jump, and Anthony Rota and Arthur Uphill of the firm of Bertram Rota Ltd whose activities on my behalf demand that they be credited as collaborators rather than booksellers.

R.S.

1940

June 1940

This early summer prepares its feasts
In the garden, hot on the blossom of the peach,
Fountaining bird song, criss-crossed with bees,
Electric with lizards, packed tight in leaves,
        And the grey First War voices, each to each

Speak, adrift on deck chairs. They say
How little they know of the war not far away,
So different from the mud of France in their day.

Beyond the glaring paths, the blowing
Dust on dog roses in hedges,
Meadows heavy with elms, dusk bringing
Sunday-pressed youths to girls, bicycling
Round War Memorials in villages;

Beyond the tranced summer sea – lines
Cut by keels on its endless glass –
Waves ever moving seeming ever still,
Tiring the day with their permanence of dance,
Beyond the steel Channel like scissors,
Snipping and snipping England from France;

        Yes! Beyond those French cliffs, a sound rolls
Ingathering murmurs from inland hills
Sound of caterpillar-wheeled blond dreams,
Sound of songs cast in steel, mechanically roaring
Above the larks' nests of France.

        'False is the feast this summer – all one garden –
Spreads before our eyes. We must harden.'

'Not the Ear nor the Eye but the Will
Is the organ which alone can make us whole.
Man's world is no more Nature. It is hell
Made by Man-self of which Man must grow well.'

'History is a dragon under human skin.
We must make friends with that evil, if we are to win.'

'Twinned with our lives was our doom
Our killer at our birth, from the same womb.'

'Our indolent injustice, for so long
Snoring over Germany, is overthrown.
To face us with an even greater wrong.'

'So be it, then! The greater wrong must meet
From the less evil, with the worse defeat.'

Afloat on the lawn, the ghostly last war voices
Gaze for a moment through their serge-grey eyes at this:
England chained to the abyss.

Then, wearied unto death, they begin
In disillusioned chorus: 'We shall win!'

But the ghost of one who was young and died,
In the cross-fire of two wars, through the faint leaves
sighed:

'I am cold as a cold world alone
Voyaging through space without faith or aim
And no Star whose rays point a Cross to believe in,
And an endless, empty need to atone.'

c. 1942   STEPHEN SPENDER

Watching Post

A hill flank overlooking the Axe valley.
Among the stubble a farmer and I keep watch
For whatever may come to injure our countryside –
Light-signals, parachutes, bombs, or sea-invaders.
The moon looks over the hill's shoulder, and hope
Mans the old ramparts of an English night.

In a house down there was Marlborough born. One night
Monmouth marched to his ruin out of that valley.
Beneath our castled hill, where Britons kept watch,
Is a church where the Drakes, old lords of this country-
    side,
Sleep under their painted effigies. No invaders
Can dispute their legacy of toughness and hope.

Two counties away, over Bristol, the searchlights hope
To find what danger is in the air tonight.
Presently gunfire from Portland reaches our valley
Tapping like an ill-hung door in a draught. My watch
Says nearly twelve. All over the countryside
Moon-dazzled men are peering out for invaders.

The farmer and I talk for a while of invaders:
But soon we turn to crops – the annual hope,
Making of cider, prizes for ewes. Tonight
How many hearts along this war-mazed valley
Dream of a day when at peace they may work and watch
The small sufficient wonders of the countryside.

Image or fact, we both in the countryside
Have found our natural law, and until invaders
Come will answer its need: for both of us, hope

Means a harvest from small beginnings, who this night
While the moon sorts out into shadow and shape our
    valley,
A farmer and a poet, are keeping watch.

July 1940   C. DAY LEWIS
c. 1943

Refugees

With prune-dark eyes, thick lips, jostling each other
These, disinterred from Europe, throng the deck
To watch their hope heave up in steel and concrete
Powerful but delicate as a swan's neck,

Thinking, each of them, the worst is over
And we do not want any more to be prominent or rich,
Only to be ourselves, to be unmolested
And make ends meet – an ideal surely which

Here if anywhere is feasible. Their glances
Like wavering antennae feel
Around the sliding limber towers of Wall Street
And count the numbered docks and gingerly steal

Into the hinterland of their own future
Behind this excessive annunciation of towers,
Tracking their future selves through a continent of
    strangeness.
The liner moves to the magnet; the quay flowers

With faces of people's friends. But these are mostly
Friendless and all they look to meet
Is a secretary who holds his levée among ledgers,
Tells them to take a chair and wait . . .

And meanwhile the city will go on, regardless
Of any new arrival, trains like prayers
Radiating from stations haughty as cathedrals,
Tableaux of spring in milliners' windows, great affairs

Being endorsed on a vulcanite table, lines of washing
Feebly garish among grimy brick and dour
Iron fire-escapes; barrows of cement are rumbling
Up airy planks; a florist adds a flower

To a bouquet that is bound for somebody's beloved
Or for someone ill; in a sombre board-room great
Problems wait to be solved or shelved. The city
Goes on but you, you will probably find, must wait

Till something or other turns up. Something-or-Other
Becomes an expected angel from the sky,
But do not trust the sky, the blue that looks so candid
Is non-committal, frigid as a harlot's eye.

Gangways – the handclasp of the land. The resurrected,
The brisk or resigned Lazaruses, who want
Another chance, go trooping ashore. But chances
Are dubious. Fate is stingy, recalcitrant

And officialdom greets them blankly as they fumble
Their foreign-looking baggage; they still feel
The movement of the ship while through their
    imagination
The known and the unheard-of constellations wheel.

New York, September 1940   LOUIS MACNEICE
p. 1941

The Dark Years

Returning each morning from a timeless world,
the senses open upon a world of time:
    after so many years the light is
  novel still and immensely ambitious,

but, translated from her own informal world,
the ego is bewildered and does not want
    a shining novelty this morning,
  and does not like the noise or the people.

For behind the doors of this ambitious day
stand shadows with enormous grudges, outside
    its chartered ocean of perception
  misshapen coastguards drunk with foreboding,

and whispering websters, creeping through this world,
discredit so much literature and praise.
    Summer was worse than we expected:
  now an Autumn cold comes on the water,

as lesser lives retire on their savings, their
small deposits of starches and nuts, and soon
    will be asleep or travelling
  or dead. But this year the towns of our childhood

are changing complexion along with the woods,
and many who have shared our conduct will add
    their pinches of detritus to the
  nutritive chain of determined being,

and even our uneliminated decline
to a vita minima, huddling for warmth,
    the hard and the soft-mouthed together
  in a coma of waiting, just breathing

in a darkness of tribulation and death,
while blizzards havoc the garden and the old
    Folly becomes unsafe, the mill-wheels
  rust, and the weirs fall slowly to pieces.

Will the inflamed ego attempt as before,
to migrate again to her family place,
    to the hanging gardens of Eros
  and the moons of a magical summer?

The local train does not run any more,
the heretical roses have lost their scent,
    and her Cornish Hollow of tryst is
  swarming now with discourteous villains

whom Father's battered hat cannot wave away,
and the fancy-governed sequence leads us all
    back to the labyrinth where either
  we are found or lose ourselves for ever.

What signs ought we to make to be found, how can
we will the knowledge that we must know to will?
    The waste is a suburb of prophets,
  but who has seen Jesus and who only

Judas the Abyss? The rocks are big and bad,
death all too substantial in the thinning air,
    learning screams in the narrow gate where
  events are traded with time but cannot

tell what logic must and must not leave to fate,
or what laws we are permitted to obey:
    there are no birds now, predatory
  glaciers glitter in a chilly evening,

and death is probable. Nevertheless,
whatever the situation and the blame,

let the lips make formal contrition
for whatever is going to happen,

time remembered bear witness to time required,
the positive and negative ways through time
    embrace and encourage each other
in a brief moment of intersection,

that the spirit orgulous may while it can
conform to its temporal focus with praise,
    acknowledging the attributes of
one immortal, one infinite Substance,

and the shabby structure of indolent flesh
give a resonant echo to the Word which was
    from the beginning, and the shining
Light be comprehended by the darkness.

p. 1941   W. H. AUDEN

'THE EARTH IS PATIENT...'

Elegy I

My pig-faced kingdom with tongues of wrong
And an historical gait of trial and error,
Under whose bridges Time, faster than rivers,
Bears individual and event along
Into a past overloaded with souvenirs:

Now answer History with a marvellous golden yes
As she steps up asking all possible questions;
The historians in their tombs, sighing, will sleep
Deeper, and the sailors, who always had great visions,
Smile for the island that ceased to be an illusion.

The instinct of the bird governs its acts of war,
Who, tittivating itself at cross-roads, rises and rises
Singing from the galaxial wheels that come roaring towards it, and in the end, after the reverses,
Perches whistling on the shattered axles proudly.

The armies of Hohenzollern, brooding on loss,
Know best that the real enemy is never there
Pinned akimbo on the gunsight, but in the cause.
O sheeted in their horoscopes like togas
Under red stars strut the catchpenny Caesars.

Heroes who ride your wishing horses over
The breakfast tables of the population,
Your beds are full of hands. And when you shiver
What stalks across your grave is a whole nation.
And when you close an eye your life is over.

But the conquerors, reddening their heels on us,
They will not ever really die but continually

Thrash on the hotbed of their terrible onus:
Not one shall die hopefully and finally,
For them the tomb will also be full of us.

c. 1943   GEORGE BARKER

Inheritance

This which I write now
Was written years ago
Before my birth
In the features of my father.

It was stamped
In the rock formations
West of my hometown.
Not I write,

But, perhaps, William Bruce
Cooper.
Perhaps here his hand
Well articled in his trade.

Then though my words
Hit out
An ebullition from
City or flower

There not my faith.
These the paint
Smeared upon
The inarticulate

– The salt crusted sea-boot,
The red eyed mackerel,
The plate shining with herring,
And many men,

Seamen and craftsmen and curers,
And behind them
The protest of hundreds of years,
The sea obstinate against the land.

p. 1943   GEORGE BRUCE

To My Father

Yes as alike as entirely
You my father I see
That high Greenock tenement
And whole shipyarded front.

As alike as a memory early
Of 'The Bonny Earl o' Moray'
Fiddled in our high kitchen
Over the sleeping town

These words this one night
Feed us and will not
Leave us without our natures
Inheriting new fires.

The March whinfires let fall
From the high Greenock hill
A word fetched so bright
Out of the forehead that

51

A fraction's wink and I
And my death change round softly.
My birth and I so softly
Change round the outward journey.

Entirely within the fires
And winter-harried natures
Of your each year, the still
Foundered man is the oracle

Tented within his early
Friendships. And he'll reply
To us locked in our song.
This night this word falling

Across the kindling skies
Takes over over our bodies.

c. 1949   W. S. GRAHAM

Cricket at Brighton

At night the Front like coloured barley-sugar; but now
Soft blue, all soda, the air goes flat over flower-beds,
Blue railings and beaches. Below, half-painted boats, bow
Up, settle in sand, names like Moss-Rose and Dolphin
Drying in a breeze that flicks at the ribs of the tide.
The chalk coastline folds up its wings of Beachy Head
And Worthing, fluttering white over water like brides.
Regency squares, the Pavilion, oysters and mussels and
  gin.

Piers like wading confectionery, esplanades of striped
  tulip.

Cricket began here yesterday, the air heavy, suitable
For medium-paced bowlers. Deck-chairs, though,
　　mostly were vacant,
Faces white over startling green. Later, trains will
　　decant
People with baskets, litter and opinions, the seaside's
　　staple
Ingredients. To-day Langridge pushes the ball for
　　unfussed
Singles; ladies clap from check rugs, talk to retired
　　colonels.
On tomato-red verandas the scoring rate is discussed.

Sussex *v.* Lancashire, the air birded and green after rain,
Dew on syringa and cherry. Seaward the water
Is satin, pale emerald, fretted with lace at the edges,
The whole sky rinsed easy like nerves after pain.
May here is childhood, lost somewhere between and
　　never
Recovered, but again moved nearer, as a lever
Turned on the pier flickers the Past into pictures.
A time of immediacy, optimism, without stricture.

Postcards and bathing-machines and old prints.
Something comes back, the inkling, the momentary hint
Of what we had wanted to be, though differently now,
For the conditions are different and what we had
　　wanted
We wanted as we were then, without conscience,
　　unhaunted,
And given the chance must refuse to want it again,
Only, occasionally, we escape, we return where we were:
Watching cricket at Brighton, Cornford bowling
　　through sea-scented air.

　　p. 1942　　　　　　　　　　　　　　ALAN ROSS

Victorian Paperweight

Over a solid glassy sky
Three paper seagulls feign to fly,
And far below their pinions, sand
Slips into shapes of sea and land.
Pale panoramic views appear,
Grey ferns are glued, prim palms displayed,
Glades umbelliferous, and here
Balmoral, there an esplanade,
A pier,
A park, a wagonette,
All paper, pressed and pasted, yet
Sap once suffused those creepers till
They screened the skies, and once the frill
Ran round the sofa's genteel foot,
And blossoms rushed from every root,
With blowsy flowers to paint the wall,
Lilies on tombs, buds for a ball,
All sprouting, bursting, falling, all
Throwing their seeds to spring and blow;
But now
No leaves are green, no more can grow.
And with how
Envious sighs we capture just
The grave's uninteresting dust.
All fearful darkness, all exceeding light
Resolve to this dull uniformity;
Their stars have paled, their yellow sun is quite
Gone down, their unreflecting ocean, dry.
Behind the sun's broad back
No black
Mysterious voids now veil a God who might
Loose His just lightnings from the midnight sky.
Our night

Is rather threaded by the throbbing flight
Of fact, from which no morning brings respite.
Now we forget how leisured years unfurled
The seasons and their fruits across the world
Like a red velvet carpet for the few
Who passed
And never knew
How fast it vanished underneath their tread
Till our glass dome was shattered overhead.

p. 1942   JANE MOORE

Pastorale

I came from Merthyr by the Cefn road
Above the crosses in the valley on
Into the uncertain nodding of the sun.
Gently we rubbed the shoulders
Burned on the brown divide
Fingering the gloss into the skin
Liquid with scuds of cloud running
Before the imperious light.
Late on its hillock spring and all the lakes
Were breaking with a toss and fret.

Inside the bus the sun drove too
Faint with a forgotten smell of leather
And clothes in coffer. Here close were Cefn folk
Keeping their limber legs for summer hours,
Then hill-farm girls, red heavy cheeks
And struggling bags, an urchin clinging
With the bread at heel.
Press double at the bell and Daio knew them all

With corny wit from crumpled schoolboy cap
To Mrs Morris and her heavy legs,
Parcel for the Twmp and tell old Danny
Three o'clock bus on Friday.
                              So the world
Up to the northern neck
Was bickered into sympathy
And run up every punctuated ridge.

Beyond the Storey Arms the bus ran down
Swinging on hairwide curves above
A wilderness. Silence was here
And sun and the smooth hum
Of tyres. The heat made
Waspish arcs of sound skid off the hill
And with it rode
The faint unkemptness of the horse.

Soon it began again, the farms below
And Daio's bell to ring the engulfing act.
'Fine for the market mun', the double touch
Went nicking in
With every name as pat
As fifteen miles away.
Downward through Libanus old ladies then
And boys with sixpence clutching hotly at the hand
To cross the bridge. Conductor saunters to
His mother's door and disappears.
At home to Daio like the hills.

So to the pinprick roofs and
Voiding the motif, voices, mountain sun
We pressed a hundred springs across the pool,
Clipping our odorous texture with a punctual knife,
Dragging the toga of the higgledy town.

p. 1944   ROLAND MATHIAS

Out of the Hills

Dreams clustering thick on his sallow skull,
Dark as curls, he comes, ambling with his cattle
From the starved pastures. He has shaken from off his
    shoulders
The weight of the sky, and the lash of the wind's sharp-
    ness
Is healing already under the medicinal sun.
Clouds of cattle breath, making the air heady,
Remember the summer's sweetness, the wet road runs
Blue as a river before him; the legendary town
Dreams of his coming; under the half-closed lids
Of the indolent shops sleep dawdles, emptying the last
Tankards of darkness, before the officious light
Bundles it up the chimney out of sight.

The shadow of the mountain dwindles; his scaly eye
Sloughs its cold care and glitters. The day is his
To dabble a finger in, and merry as crickets,
A chorus of coins sings in his tattered pockets.
Shall we follow him down, witness his swift undoing
In the indifferent streets: the sudden disintegration
Of his soul's hardness, traditional discipline
Of flint and frost thawing in ludicrous showers
Of maudlin laughter; the limpid runnels of speech
Sullied and slurred, as the beer-glass chimes the hours?
No, wait for him here. At midnight he will return,
Threading the tunnel that contains the dawn
Of all his fears. Be then his fingerpost
Homeward. The earth is patient; he is not lost.

c. 1946   R. S. THOMAS

A Peasant

Iago Prytherch his name, though, be it allowed,
Just an ordinary man of the bald Welsh hills,
Who pens a few sheep in a gap of cloud.
Docking mangels, chipping the green skin
From the yellow bones with a half-witted grin
Of satisfaction, or churning the crude earth
To a stiff sea of clods that glint in the wind –
So are his days spent, his spittled mirth
Rarer than the sun that cracks the cheeks
Of the gaunt sky perhaps once in a week.
And then at night see him fixed in his chair
Motionless, except when he leans to gob in the fire.
There is something frightening in the vacancy of his mind.
His clothes, sour with years of sweat
And animal contact, shock the refined,
But affected, sense with their stark naturalness.
Yet this is your prototype, who, season by season
Against siege of rain and the wind's attrition,
Preserves his stock, an impregnable fortress
Not to be stormed even in death's confusion.
Remember him, then, for he, too, is a winner of wars,
Enduring like a tree under the curious stars.

p. 1944   R. S. THOMAS

Personal History

FOR MY SON

O my heart is the unlucky heir of the ages,
And my body is unwillingly the secret agent
Of my ancestors; those content with their wages
From history: the Cumberland Quaker whose gentle
Face was framed with lank hair to hide the ears
Cropped as a punishment for his steadfast faith,
The Spanish lady who had seen the pitch lake's broth
In the West Indian island and the Fife farmers
To whom the felted barley meant a winter's want.

My face presents my history, and its sallow skin
Is parchment for the Edinburgh lawyer's deed:
To have and hold in trust, as feeofee therein
Until such date as the owner shall have need
Thereof. My brown eyes are jewels I cannot pawn,
And my long lip once curled beside an Irish bog,
My son's whorled ear was once my father's, then mine;
I am the map of a campaign, each ancestor has his flag
Marking an advance or a retreat. I am their seed.

As I write I look at the five fingers of my hand,
Each with its core of nacre bone, and rippled nails;
Turn to the palm and the traced unequal lines that end
In death – only at the tips my ancestry fails –
The dotted swirls are original and are my own:
Look at this fringed polyp which I daily use
And ask its history, ask to what grave abuse
It has been put: perhaps it curled about the stone
Of Cain. At least it has known much of evil,

And perhaps as much of good, been tender
When tenderness was needed, and been firm

On occasion, and in its past been free of gender,
Been the hand of a mother holding the warm
Impress of the child against her throbbing breast,
Been cool to the head inflamed in fever,
Sweet and direct in contact with a lover.
O in its cupped and fluted shell lies all the past,
My fingers close about the crash of history's storm.

In the tent of night I hear the voice of Calvin
Expending his hatred of the world in icy words;
Man less than a red ant beneath the towering mountain,
And God a troll more fearful than the feudal lords:
The Huguenots in me, flying St Bartholomew's Day,
Are in agreement with all this, and their resentful hate
Flames brighter than the candles on an altar, the grey
Afternoon is lit by catherine wheels of terror, the street
Drinks blood, and pity is death before their swords.

The cantilever of my bones acknowledges the architect,
My father, to whom always the world was a mystery
Concealed in the humped base of a bottle, one solid fact
To set against the curled pages and the tears of history.
I am a Border keep, a croft and a solicitor's office,
A country rectory, a farm and a drawing board:
In me, as in so many, the past has stowed its miser's hoard,
Won who knows where nor with what loaded dice.
When my blood pulses it is their blood I feel hurry.

These forged me, the latest link in a fertile chain
With ends that run so far that my short sight
Cannot follow them, nor can my weak memory claim
Acquaintance with the earliest shackle. In my height
And breadth I hold my history, and then my son
Holds my history in his small body and the history of
   another,

Who for me has no contact but that of flesh, his mother.
What I make now I make, indeed, from the unknown,
A blind man spinning furiously in the web of night.

p. 1940   RUTHVEN TODD

Cockley Moor, Dockray, Penrith

Outside, the cubist fells are drawn again
Beneath the light that speaks ex tempore;
The fur of bracken thickens in the rain
And wrinkles shift upon the scurfy scree.

Inside, like tiles the poet's pleasures lie,
Square laid on circle, circle laid on square,
And pencilled angles of eternity
Are calculated on the doubled stair.

Outside, the curlew gargles through the mist,
The mountain pansies shut up shop and fade,
The wheatear chisels with his crystal fist,
And day on day like stone on stone is laid.

Inside, are cows on canvas, painted boom
Fresh as a girl's thin fingers burst to flower,
Bright leaves that do not fall, but fence the room
With the arrested growth of a June hour.

The curving cloud embellishes the sky,
The geometric rain slants to the corn;
Inside, a man remembers he must die,
Outside, a stone forgets that it was born.

c. 1944   NORMAN NICHOLSON

61

Tyne Dock

The summer season at Tyne Dock
Lifted my boyhood in a crane
Above the shaggy mining town,
Above the slaghills and the rocks,
Above the middens in backlanes
And wooden hen-huts falling down.

Grass grew vermilion in the streets
Where the blind pit-ponies pranced
And poppies screamed by butchers' stalls
Where bulls kicked sparks with dying feet,
And in the naked larks I sensed
A cruel god beneath it all.

Over the pithead wheel the moon
Was clean as a girl's face in school;
I envied the remote old man
Who lived there, quiet and alone,
While in the kitchen the mad spool
Unwound, as Annie's treadle ran.

Squat fishing-smacks swung down the Tyne
And windwards their wide tan sails spread
With bobbling lights red on the wave,
While with their lanterns to the mine
The pitmen clogged, and by my bed
Night kneeled, and all the day forgave.

The boyish season is still there
For clapping hands and leaping feet
Across the slagheaps and the dunes,
And still it breaks into my care

Though I will never find the street,
Nor find the old, impulsive tune,
Nor ever lose that child's despair.

p. 1947   FRANCIS SCARFE

Corfe Castle

Framed in a jagged window of grey stones
These wooded pastures have a dream-like air.
You thrill with disbelief
To see the cattle move in a green field.

Grey Purbeck houses by the sun deceived
Sleep with the easy conscience of the old;
The swathes are sweet on slopes new harvested;
Householders prune their gardens, count the slugs;
The beanrows flicker flowers red as flames.

Those to whom life is a picture card
Get their cheap thrill where here the centuries stand
A thrusting mass transfigured by the sun
Reeling above the streets and crowing farms.
The rooks and skylarks are O.K. for sound,
The toppling bastions innocent with stock.

Love grows impulsive here: the best forget;
The failures of the earth will try again.
She would go back to him if he but asked.

The tawny thrush is silent; when he sings
His silence is fulfilled. Who wants to talk
As trippers do? Yet, love,

Before we go be simple as this grass.
Lie rustling for this last time in my arms.
Quicken the dying island with your breath.

p. 1942   ALUN LEWIS

Stormy Day

O look how the loops and balloons of bloom
Bobbing on long strings from the finger-ends
And knuckles of the lurching cherry-tree
Heap and hug, elbow and part, this wild day,
Like a careless carillon cavorting;
And the beaded whips of the beeches splay
And dip like anchored weed round a drowned rock,
And hovering effortlessly the rooks
Hang on the wind's effrontery as if
On hooks, then loose their hold and slide away
Like sleet sidewards down the warm swimming sweep
Of wind. O it is a lovely time when
Out of the sunk and rigid sumps of thought
Our hearts rise and race with new sounds and sights
And signs, tingling delightedly at the sting
And crunch of springless carts on gritty roads,
The caught kite dangling in the skinny wires,
The swipe of a swallow across the eyes,
Striped awnings stretched on lawns. New things surprise
And stop us everywhere. In the parks
The fountains scoop and flower like rockets
Over the oval ponds whose even skin
Is pocked and goosefleshed by their niggling rain
That frocks a naked core of statuary.
And at jetty's jut, roped and ripe for hire,
The yellow boats lie yielding and lolling,

Jilted and jolted like jellies. But look!
There! Do you see, crucified on palings,
Motionless news-posters announcing
That now the frozen armies melt and meet
And smash! Go home now, for, try as you may,
You will not shake off that fact to-day.
Behind you limps that dog with tarry paw,
As behind him, perfectly-timed, follows
The dumb shadow that mimes him all the way.

p. 1940   W. R. RODGERS

Early March

We did not expect this; we were not ready for this; –
To find the unpredicted spring
Sprung open like a broken trap. The sky
Unfolds like an arum leaf; the bare
Trees unfurl like fronds of fern;
The birds are scattered along the air;
Celandines and cresses prick pinpoints white and yellow,
And the snow is stripped from the fells.
We were not prepared for this. We knew
That the avalanche of war breaks boundaries like birches,
That terror bursts round our roofs; we were aware
Of the soft cough of death in the waiting lungs. But this
Has caught us half-asleep. We had never thought of this.

c. 1948   NORMAN NICHOLSON

Day of These Days

Such a morning it is when love
leans through geranium windows
and calls with a cockerel's tongue.

When red-haired girls scamper like roses
over the rain-green grass;
and the sun drips honey.

When hedgerows grow venerable,
berries dry black as blood,
and holes suck in their bees.

Such a morning it is when mice
run whispering from the church,
dragging dropped ears of harvest.

When the partridge draws back his spring
and shoots like a buzzing arrow
over grained and mahogany fields.

When no table is bare,
and no beast dry,
and the tramp feeds on ribs of rabbit.

Such a day it is when time
piles up the hills like pumpkins,
and the streams run golden.

When all men smell good,
and the cheeks of girls
are as baked bread to the mouth.

66

As bread and beanflowers
the touch of their lips,
and their white teeth sweeter than cucumbers.

p. 1946   LAURIE LEE

Midsummer 1942

Clear and brilliant the moss flowers
yellow in tuft and clump on weathered stone,
on roof, on walls in the sun:
short, haired stalks and exact stars
in the still heat, the noon.

Time hangs: with languor and heat
but terribly, also, now with hatred or anger
or the void when both are spent – the dead weight
of emptiness suddenly-understood; remote
as hope, yet near and clear as hunger;

time's weight strikes us all with the small, the 'slight –'
stabbing one to awareness with the slender-bladed
reed by Libyan spring, another in Poland
numbed by rush of longing at the sight
of a straggling vetch in a hedge, or a bird's flight:

a girl in a Dorset orchard watching the trees
or a girl in a flat with a bowl of pale roses
numbed or stabbed by time that lies
so heavy in their beds
stubborn as stone, sharp as this flare of mosses.

September, and the harvest sun
on the wind-trembled willows by the stream
on waggon, sheaves and barn;

and now October afternoon:
colder, clouds winter-touched, as dusk
softens the ploughland with its misted bloom.

c. 1948   CHRISTOPHER LEE

'The dizzy summer calf . . .'

The dizzy summer calf, hen chasing sparrow,
bristle of grass, the tilted grids of waggons,
the posing mare in a violet tent of shadow –
sun burns on these; his fiery light is steep,
and the day halts and pants between step and step.

No water in this quilted country dances
or shivers in cool shocks in pots of limestone
or melts the fiery flakes with bubble flounces
or echoes birches with its shaggy fall,
but in green pools holds its own funeral.

No music now but colour, green on green;
breathless in light the wind has lost its voice;
no thrust to string the moment on a tune.
And cuckoo sounds his horn no longer from
his castle of shadow in the summer dream.

The puff of heat balled in my dancing eye
bows like a hazel twig above desire
of crisping sand and dowses for the sea,
and while a furnace moment halts and hangs
I am where water walks and wind sings.

c. 1943   NORMAN MCCAIG

April Rise

If ever I saw blessing in the air
   I see it now in this still early day
Where lemon-green the vaporous morning drips
   Wet sunlight on the powder of my eye.

Blown bubble film of blue, the sky wraps round
   Weeds of warm light whose every root and rod
Splutters with soapy green, and all the world
   Sweats with the bead of summer in its bud.

If ever I heard blessing it is there
   Where birds in trees that shoals and shadows are
Splash with their hidden wings, and drops of sound
   Break on my ears their crests of throbbing air.

Pure in the haze the emerald sun dilates,
   The lips of mosses milk the spongy stones,
While white as water by the lake a girl
   Swims her green hand among the gathered swans.

Now, as the almond burns its smoking wick,
   Dropping small flames to light the candled grass;
Now, as my low blood scales its second chance,
   If ever world were blessed, now it is.

p. 1946   LAURIE LEE

Fern Hill

Now as I was young and easy under the apple boughs
About the lilting house and happy as the grass was green,
    The night above the dingle starry,
      Time let me hail and climb
    Golden in the heydays of his eyes,
And honoured among wagons I was prince of the apple
    towns
And once below a time I lordly had the trees and leaves
      Trail with daisies and barley
    Down the rivers of the windfall light.

And as I was green and carefree, famous among the barns
About the happy yard and singing as the farm was home,
    In the sun that is young once only,
      Time let me play and be
    Golden in the mercy of his means,
And green and golden I was huntsman and herdsman,
    the calves
Sang to my horn, the foxes on the hills barked clear and
    cold,
      And the sabbath rang slowly
    In the pebbles of the holy streams.

All the sun long it was running, it was lovely, the hay
Fields high as the house, the tunes from the chimneys, it
    was air
    And playing, lovely and watery
      And fire green as grass.
    And nightly under the simple stars
As I rode to sleep the owls were bearing the farm away,
All the moon long I heard, blessed among stables, the
    nightjars

Flying with the ricks, and the horses
    Flashing into the dark.

And then to awake, and the farm, like a wanderer white
With the dew, come back, the cock on his shoulder: it was all
    Shining, it was Adam and maiden,
        The sky gathered again
   And the sun grew round that very day.
So it must have been after the birth of the simple light
In the first, spinning place, the spellbound horses walking
  warm
    Out of the whinnying green stable
     On to the fields of praise.

And honoured among foxes and pheasants by the gay
  house
Under the new made clouds and happy as the heart was
  long,
    In the sun born over and over,
        I ran my heedless ways,
    My wishes raced through the house high hay
And nothing I cared, at my sky blue trades, that time
  allows
In all his tuneful turning so few and such morning songs
    Before the children green and golden
        Follow him out of grace,

Nothing I cared, in the lamb white days, that time would
  take me
Up to the swallow thronged loft by the shadow of my hand,
    In the moon that is always rising,
       Nor that riding to sleep
   I should hear him fly with the high fields
And wake to the farm forever fled from the childless land.

Oh as I was young and easy in the mercy of his means,
Time held me green and dying
Though I sang in my chains like the sea.

p. 1945   DYLAN THOMAS

The Feather

I stoop to gather a seabird's feather
Fallen on the beach,
Torn from a beautiful drifting wing;
What can I learn or teach,
Running my finger through the comb
And along the horny quill?
The body it was torn from
Gave out a cry so shrill,
Sailors looked from their white road
To see what help was there.
It dragged the winds to a drop of blood
Falling through drowned air,
Dropping from the sea-hawk's beak,
From frenzied talons sharp;
Now if the words they lost I speak
It must be to that harp
Under the strange, light-headed sea
That bears a straw of the nest.
Unless I make that melody,
How can the dead have rest?

Sheer from wide air to the wilderness
The victim fell, and lay;
The starlike bone is fathomless,
Lost among wind and spray.

This lonely, isolated thing
Trembles amid their sound.
I set my finger on the string
That spins the ages round.
But let it sleep, let it sleep
Where shell and stone are cast;
Its ecstasy the Furies keep,
For nothing here is past.
The perfect into night must fly;
On this the winds agree.
How could a blind rock satisfy
The hungers of the sea?

c. 1948   VERNON WATKINS

The Islander

My eyes are marble
my veins are wire

It is the end of the season of growth
the olives are withered
you cannot eat the stones

The boat in the secret cove
cannot save me now
the sails untended are rags
the planks unoiled are warped

Here I stay
as the orchards rot
the branches snap under the weight of nests
there are stone eggs in the nests

73

there is nobody to bury me
the wind and the returning birds
will not mourn me

p. 1946   LAWRIE SCARLETT

Since All My Steps Taken

Since all my steps taken
Are audience of my last
With hobnail on Ben Narnain
Or mind on the word's crest
I'll walk the kyleside shingle
With scarcely a hark back
To the step dying from my heel
Or the creak of the rucksack.
All journey, since the first
Step from my father and mother
Towards the word's crest
Or walking towards that other,
The new step arrives out
Of all my steps taken
And out of today's light.
Day long I've listened for,
Like the cry of a rare bird
Blown into life in the ear,
The speech to that dead horde
Since all my steps taken
Are audience of my last
With hobnail on Ben Narnain
Or mind on the word's crest.

c. 1949   W. S. GRAHAM

Kirkwall 1942

Far again, far,
And the Pentland howling psalms of separation
Lifts and falls, lifts and falls between.
But present pain
Folds like a firth round islets that contain
A sheepfold and a single habitation –
Moments in our summer of success –
Or the greater islands, colonized and built with peace.

Cold knives of light
Make every outline clear in a northern island,
The separating light, the sea's green;
Yet southern lives
Merge in the lupin fields or sleepy coves,
In crowstepped gables find a hint of Holland,
And Europe in the red religious stone:
All places in the room where we in love lie down.

p. 1942   ANNE RIDLER

Kinnaird Head

I go North to cold, to home, to Kinnaird,
Fit monument for our time.

This is the outermost edge of Buchan.
Inland the sea birds range,
The tree's leaf has salt upon it,
The tree turns to the low stone wall.
And here a promontory rises towards Norway,

Irregular to the top of thin grey grass
Where the spindrift in storm lays its beads.
The water plugs in the cliff sides,
The gull cries from the clouds,
This is the consummation of the plain.

O impregnable and very ancient rock,
Rejecting the violence of water,
Ignoring its accumulations and strategy,
You yield to history nothing.

p. 1943   GEORGE BRUCE

William Wordsworth

No room for mourning: he's gone out
Into the noisy glen, or stands between the stones
Of the gaunt ridge, or you'll hear his shout
Rolling among the screes, he being a boy again.
He'll never fail nor die
And if they laid his bones
In the wet vaults or iron sarcophagi
Of fame, he'd rise at the first summer rain
And stride across the hills to seek
His rest among the broken lands and clouds.
He was a stormy day, a granite peak
Spearing the sky; and look, about its base
Words flower like crocuses in the hanging woods,
Blank though the dalehead and the bony face.

September 1941   SIDNEY KEYES
c. 1945

Rock Face

In the quarry
I found the face – brow and nose and eyes
Cleft in a stare of ten-year-old surprise,
With slate lids slid backwards, grass and plantain
Tufted in ear and nostril, and an ooze
Like drip from marble mouth that spews
Into the carved trough of a city fountain.
Now the rock is blasted, and the dub
Chock-full of soil and rubble, and the shale
Carried away in cart and lorry,
Yet still like cracked reflections in a pool,
Or image broken in a smithereen of mirrors,
Or picture jigged and sawn with paste and scissors,
The rock face, temple, mouth and all,
Peers bleakly at me from this dry-stone wall.

c. 1948   NORMAN NICHOLSON

Spring Song, *1948*

Let it be recorded for those who come after,
If any are left to come after, that today
Streams melted on the moor, a curlew's song
Wept in remembered sunshine and the long
Cloud-shadows dipped away
Where the west wind blew softer.

O in the black frost of the world's December,
In the cold shadow of our stricken years
Who have small reason, now, to laugh or play,

77

Set down, set down that this was a spring day
To be remembered with tears,
If any are left to remember.

c. 1949   PAUL DEHN

Poem in October

It was my thirtieth year to heaven
Woke to my hearing from harbour and neighbour wood
And the mussel pooled and the heron
Priested shore
The morning beckon
With water praying and call of seagull and rook
And the knock of sailing boats on the net webbed wall
Myself to set foot
That second
In the still sleeping town and set forth.

My birthday began with the water-
Birds and the birds of the winged trees flying my name
Above the farms and the white horses
And I rose
In rainy autumn
And walked abroad in a shower of all my days.
High tide and the heron dived when I took the road
Over the border
And the gates
Of the town closed as the town awoke.

A springful of larks in a rolling
Cloud and the roadside bushes brimming with whistling
Blackbirds and the sun of October
Summery
On the hill's shoulder,

Here were fond climates and sweet singers suddenly
Come in the morning where I wandered and listened
To the rain wringing
Wind blow cold
In the wood faraway under me.

Pale rain over the dwindling harbour
And over the sea wet church the size of a snail
With its horns through mist and the castle
Brown as owls
But all the gardens
Of spring and summer were blooming in the tall tales
Beyond the border and under the lark full cloud.
There could I marvel
My birthday
Away but the weather turned around.

It turned away from the blithe country
And down the other air and the blue altered sky
Streamed again a wonder of summer
With apples
Pears and red currants
And I saw the turning so clearly a child's
Forgotten mornings when he walked with his mother
Through the parables
Of sun light
And the legends of the green chapels

And the twice told fields of infancy
That his tears burned my cheeks and his heart moved in
mine.
These were the woods the river and sea
Where a boy
In the listening
Summertime of the dead whispered the truth of his joy
To the trees and the stones and the fish in the tide.

And the mystery
Sang alive
Still in the water and singing birds.

And there could I marvel my birthday
Away but the weather turned around. And the true
Joy of the long dead child sang burning
In the sun.
It was my thirtieth
Year to heaven stood there then in the summer noon
Though the town below lay leaved with October blood.
O may my heart's truth
Still be sung
On this high hill in a year's turning.

p. 1945   DYLAN THOMAS

Listen. Put on Morning

Listen. Put on morning.
Waken into falling light.
A man's imagining
Suddenly may inherit
The handclapping centuries
Of his one minute on earth.
And hear the virgin juries
Talk with his own breath
To the corner boys of his street.
And hear the Black Maria
Searching the town at night.
And hear the playropes caa
The sister Mary in.
And hear Willie and Davie
Among bracken of Narnain

Sing in a mist heavy
With myrtle and listeners.
And hear the higher town
Weep a petition of fears
At the poorhouse close upon
The public heartbeat.
And hear the children tig
And run with my own feet
Into the netting drag
Of a suiciding principle.
Listen. Put on lightbreak.
Waken into miracle.
The audience lies awake
Under the tenements
Under the sugar docks
Under the printed moments.
The centuries turn their locks
And open under the hill
Their inherited books and doors
All gathered to distil
Like happy berry pickers
One voice to talk to us.
Yes listen. It carries away
The second and the years
Till the heart's in a jacket of snow
And the head's in a helmet white
And the song sleeps to be wakened
By the morning ear bright.
Listen. Put on morning.
Waken into falling light.

c. 1949   W. S. GRAHAM

'THAT BATTLE-FIT WE LIVED...'

A Wartime Dawn

Dulled by the slow glare of the yellow bulb;
As far from sleep still as at any hour
Since distant midnight; with a hollow skull
In which white vapours seem to reel
Among limp muddles of old thought; till eyes
Collapse into themselves like clams in mud . . .
Hand paws the wall to reach the chilly switch;
Then nerve-shot darkness gradually shakes
Throughout the room. *Lie still* . . . Limbs twitch;
Relapse to immobility's faint ache. And time
A while relaxes; space turns wholly black.

But deep in the velvet crater of the ear
A chip of sound abruptly irritates.
A second, a third chirp; and then another far
Emphatic trill and chirrup shrills in answer; notes
From all directions round pluck at the strings
Of hearing with frail finely-sharpened claws.
And in an instant, every wakened bird
Across surrounding miles of air
Outside, is sowing like a scintillating sand
Its throat's incessantly replenished store
Of tuneless singsong, timeless, aimless, blind.

Draw now with prickling hand the curtains back;
Unpin the blackout-cloth; let in
Grim crack-of-dawn's first glimmer through the glass.
All's yet half sunk in Yesterday's stale death,
Obscurely still beneath a moist-tinged blank
Sky like the inside of a deaf mute's mouth . . .
Nearest within the window's sight, ash-pale
Against a cinder-coloured wall, the white

Pear-blossom hovers like a stare; rain-wet
The further housetops weakly shine; and there,
Beyond, hangs flaccidly a lone barrage-balloon.

An incommunicable desolation weighs
Like depths of stagnant water on this break of day. –
Long meditation without thought. – Until a breeze
From some pure Nowhere straying, stirs
A pang of poignant odour from the earth, an unheard sigh
Pregnant with sap's sweet tang and raw soil's fine
Aroma, smell of stone, and acrid breath
Of gravel puddles. While the brooding green
Of nearby gardens' grass and trees, and quiet flat
Blue leaves, the distant lilac mirages, are made
Clear by increasing daylight, and intensified.

Now head sinks into pillows in retreat
Before this morning's hovering advance;
(Behind loose lids, in sleep's warm porch, half hears
White hollow clink of bottles, – dragging crunch
Of milk-cart wheels, – and presently a snatch
Of windy whistling as the newsboy's bike winds near,
Distributing to neighbour's peaceful steps
Reports of last-night's battles); at last sleeps.
While early guns on Norway's bitter coast
Where faceless troops are landing, renew fire:
And one more day of War starts everywhere.

April 1940   DAVID GASCOYNE
c. 1943

86

All Day It Has Rained . . .

All day it has rained, and we on the edge of the moors
Have sprawled in our bell-tents, moody and dull as
    boors,
Groundsheets and blankets spread on the muddy ground
And from the first grey wakening we have found
No refuge from the skirmishing fine rain
And the wind that made the canvas heave and flap
And the taut wet guy-ropes ravel out and snap.
All day the rain has glided, wave and mist and dream,
Drenching the gorse and heather, a gossamer stream
Too light to stir the acorns that suddenly
Snatched from their cups by the wild south-westerly
Pattered against the tent and our upturned dreaming
    faces.
And we stretched out, unbuttoning our braces,
Smoking a Woodbine, darning dirty socks,
Reading the Sunday papers – I saw a fox
And mentioned it in the note I scribbled home; –
And we talked of girls, and dropping bombs on Rome,
And thought of the quiet dead and the loud celebrities
Exhorting us to slaughter, and the herded refugees;
– Yet thought softly, morosely of them, and as indifferently
As of ourselves or those whom we
For years have loved, and will again
Tomorrow maybe love; but now it is the rain
Possesses us entirely, the twilight and the rain.

And I can remember nothing dearer or more to my heart
Than the children I watched in the woods on Saturday
Shaking down burning chestnuts for the schoolyard's
    merry play,
Or the shaggy patient dog who followed me

By Sheet and Steep and up the wooded scree
To the Shoulder o' Mutton where Edward Thomas
  brooded long
On death and beauty – till a bullet stopped his song.

c. 1942   ALUN LEWIS

Lessons of the War

TO ALAN MICHELL

Vixi duellis nuper idoneus
Et militavi non sine gloria

I. NAMING OF PARTS

Today we have naming of parts. Yesterday,
We had daily cleaning. And tomorrow morning,
We shall have what to do after firing. But today,
Today we have naming of parts. Japonica
Glistens like coral in all of the neighbouring gardens,
    And today we have naming of parts.

This is the lower sling swivel. And this
Is the upper sling swivel, whose use you will see,
When you are given your slings. And this is the piling
  swivel,
Which in your case you have not got. The branches
Hold in the gardens their silent, eloquent gestures,
    Which in our case we have not got.

This is the safety-catch, which is always released
With an easy flick of the thumb. And please do not let me
See anyone using his finger. You can do it quite easy

88

If you have any strength in your thumb. The blossoms
Are fragile and motionless, never letting anyone see
    Any of them using their finger.

And this you can see is the bolt. The purpose of this
Is to open the breech, as you see. We can slide it
Rapidly backwards and forwards: we call this
Easing the spring. And rapidly backwards and forwards
The early bees are assaulting and fumbling the flowers:
    They call it easing the Spring.

They call it easing the Spring: it is perfectly easy
If you have any strength in your thumb: like the bolt,
And the breech, and the cocking-piece, and the point of
    balance,
Which in our case we have not got; and the almond-
    blossom
Silent in all of the gardens and the bees going backwards
    and forwards,
    For today we have naming of parts.

II. JUDGING DISTANCES

Not only how far away, but the way that you say it
Is very important. Perhaps you may never get
The knack of judging a distance, but at least you know
How to report on a landscape: the central sector,
The right of arc and that, which we had last Tuesday,
    And at least you know

That maps are of time, not place, so far as the army
Happens to be concerned – the reason being,
Is one which need not delay us. Again, you know
There are three kinds of tree, three only, the fir and the
    poplar,

And those which have bushy tops to; and lastly
    That things only seem to be things.

A barn is not called a barn, to put it more plainly,
Or a field in the distance, where sheep may be safely
    grazing.
You must never be over-sure. You must say, when
    reporting:
At five o'clock in the central sector is a dozen
Of what appear to be animals; whatever you do,
    Don't call the bleeders *sheep*.

I am sure that's quite clear; and suppose, for the sake of
    example,
The one at the end, asleep, endeavours to tell us
What he sees over there to the west, and how far away,
After first having come to attention. There to the west,
On the fields of summer the sun and the shadows bestow
    Vestments of purple and gold.

The still white dwellings are like a mirage in the heat,
And under the swaying elms a man and a woman
Lie gently together. Which is, perhaps, only to say
That there is a row of houses to the left of arc,
And that under some poplars a pair of what appear to be
    humans
    Appear to be loving.

Well that, for an answer, is what we might rightly call
Moderately satisfactory only, the reason being,
Is that two things have been omitted, and those are
    important.
The human beings, now: in what direction are they,
And how far away, would you say? And do not forget
    There may be dead ground in between.

There may be dead ground in between; and I may not
   have got
The knack of judging a distance; I will only venture
A guess that perhaps between me and the apparent lovers,
(Who, incidentally, appear by now to have finished,)
At seven o'clock from the houses, is roughly a distance
     Of about one year and a half.

III. UNARMED COMBAT

In due course of course you will all be issued with
Your proper issue; but until tomorrow,
You can hardly be said to need it; and until that time,
We shall have unarmed combat. I shall teach you.
The various holds and rolls and throws and breakfalls
     Which you may sometimes meet.

And the various holds and rolls and throws and breakfalls
Do not depend on any sort of weapon,
But only on what I might coin a phrase and call
The ever-important question of human balance,
And the ever-important need to be in a strong
     Position at the start.

There are many kinds of weakness about the body,
Where you would least expect, like the ball of the foot.
But the various holds and rolls and throws and breakfalls
Will always come in useful. And never be frightened
To tackle from behind: it may not be clean to do so,
     But this is global war.

So give them all you have, and always give them
As good as you get; it will always get you somewhere.
(You may not know it, but you can tie a Jerry
Up without rope; it is one of the things I shall teach you.)

Nothing will matter if only you are ready for him.
    The readiness is all.

The readiness is all. How can I help but feel
I have been here before? But somehow then,
I was the tied-up one. How to get out
Was always then my problem. And even if I had
A piece of rope I was always the sort of person
    Who threw the rope aside.

And in my time I have given them all I had,
Which was never as good as I got, and it got me nowhere.
And the various holds and rolls and throws and breakfalls
Somehow or other I always seemed to put
In the wrong place. And as for war, my wars
    Were global from the start.

Perhaps I was never in a strong position,
Or the ball of my foot got hurt, or I had some weakness
Where I had least expected. But I think I see your point.
While awaiting a proper issue, we must learn the lesson
Of the ever-important question of human balance.
    It is courage that counts.

Things may be the same again; and we must fight
Not in the hope of winning but rather of keeping
Something alive: so that when we meet our end,
It may be said that we tackled wherever we could,
That battle-fit we lived, and though defeated,
    Not without glory fought.

c. 1946   HENRY REED

London Before Invasion: 1940

Walls and buildings stand here still, like shells.
Hold them to the ear. There are no echoes even
Of the seas that once were. That tide is out
Beyond the valleys and hills.

Days dawn and die while the city assumes a distance of
    stars.
It is the absence of the heart
In the ebbing seas of heaven,
An ebbing beyond laughter and too tense for tears.

Now, imagination floats, a weed, on water's vacancy.
Faces of women, lit with conscience past or future
Of men gone, wear one garland of stone features.
Flowers have a girl's irrelevance, and mind is no
    prescience.

Flood-tides returning may bring with them blood and fire,
Blenching with wet panic spirit that must be rock.
May bring a future tossed and torn, as slippery as wrack.
All time adrift in torrents of blind war.

p. 1940   J. F. HENDRY

Is There No Love Can Link Us?

Is there no thread to bind us – I and he
Who is dying now, this instant as I write
And may be cold before this line's complete?

Is there no power to link us – I and she
Across whose body the loud roof is falling?

93

Or the child, whose blackening skin
Blossoms with hideous roses in the smoke?

Is there no love can link us – I and they?
Only this hectic moment? This fierce instant
Striking now
Its universal, its uneven blow?

There is no other link. Only this sliding
Second we share: this desperate edge of now.

c. 1941   MERVYN PEAKE

London, 1941

Half masonry, half pain; her head
From which the plaster breaks away
Like flesh from the rough bone, is turned
Upon a neck of stones; her eyes
Are lid-less windows of smashed glass,
Each star-shaped pupil
Giving upon a vault so vast
How can the head contain it?

The raw smoke
Is inter-wreathing through the raggedness
Of her sky-broken panes, and mirror'd
Fires dance like madmen on the splinters.

All else is stillness save the dancing splinters
And the slow inter-wreathing of the smoke.

Her breasts are crumbling brick where the black ivy
Had clung like a fantastic child for succour

94

And now hangs draggled with long peels of paper,
Fire-crisp, fire-faded awnings of limp paper
Repeating still their ghosted leaf and lily.

Grass for her cold skin's hair, the grass of cities
Wilted and swaying on her plaster brow
From winds that sweep along the streets of cities:

Across a world of sudden fear and firelight
She towers erect, the great stones at her throat,
Her rusted ribs like railings round her heart;
A figure of wild wounds – of winter wounds –
O mother of wounds; half masonry, half pain.

c. 1941   MERVYN PEAKE

Balloon Barrage

To see these captive balloons straining for sky
Is to know, suddenly, the pull of stars,
And interstellar freedom; watch them rise,
Plunge with a dolphin glee upon the air –
As though the earth were sea-bed, hills its coral,
Its waving forests and its cornlands weed,
And air its tidals over, where they ride,
These poised fish-birds, these strange leviathans.

They nose the wind with ponderous precision,
As fish nosing a stream; steer soundlessly
Through sinking hulls, lost galleons of cloud;
Light takes them smoothly with a slanting bloom,
Softened and filtered down unfathomed space
From that far, blue, bright, unimagined place
Where sky's pure ether meets earth's topmost wave.

Silver at noonday; in the afterglow
Refracted from the sunset, flushed and flecked
Prismed and pricked with colour from the sun;
Then silhouetted on the dwindling dusk;
Till light no longer penetrates that sea,
And currents merge around them, and all's one
In dark surge and in swinging tides of night.

c. 1946   JAMES WALKER

Cycle

VI

Suddenly at night the bombers came
in the hard reverberating bowl of the sky,
destroying the factory and the tall cathedral,
the dock, the warehouse, and the railway station,
the rich house in the leafy avenue,
and the shouldering tenements of the narrow streets,
and the bodies and souls of men.

I sought my son among the smoking stones
where I had crouched with him clutched at my breast
until the bomb burst and the building shattered down
and the dark came and severed my son from me.
I cried out with a voice harsh in my throat
My son, I have lost my son.
And charred faces stared at me with pity
and I saw the city burning about me
and the flash of guns on the dark smoke
and I heard bombs burst in the fire and in my heart,
but no one came to seek my son.

I besought a man who ran among the rubble
shouting and stumbling, to stay and find my son,
but he said, There is fire in my eyes, and I am blind.
And the red hollow shells in the white face
glared at the black sky and the hard ice of the stars
where still the burden of engines nagged in the brass
bowl of night, and the stiff white searchlights stalked;
while the bombs raged down, shrieking into the city,
and the guns mumbled and barked at the thunderous sky.
And the fire blossomed among the black bones of the
    street
and rushed across the stones and took my son.

c. 1945   SEAN JENNET

A Refusal to Mourn the Death, by Fire, of a Child in London

Never until the mankind making
Bird beast and flower
Fathering and all humbling darkness
Tells with silence the last light breaking
And the still hour
Is come of the sea tumbling in harness

And I must enter again the round
Zion of the water bead
And the synagogue of the ear of corn
Shall I let pray the shadow of a sound
Or sow my salt seed
In the least valley of sackcloth to mourn

The majesty and burning of the child's death.
I shall not murder

The mankind of her going with a grave truth
Nor blaspheme down the stations of the breath
With any further
Elegy of innocence and youth.

Deep with the first dead lies London's daughter,
Robed in the long friends,
The grains beyond age, the dark veins of her mother,
Secret by the unmourning water
Of the riding Thames.
After the first death, there is no other.

c. 1945   DYLAN THOMAS

To My Mother

Most near, most dear, most loved and most far,
Under the window where I often found her
Sitting as huge as Asia, seismic with laughter,
Gin and chicken helpless in her Irish hand,
Irresistible as Rabelais, but most tender for
The lame dogs and hurt birds that surround her, –
She is a procession no one can follow after
But be like a little dog following a brass band.

She will not glance up at the bomber, or condescend
To drop her gin and scuttle to a cellar,
But lean on the mahogany table like a mountain
Whom only faith can move, and so I send
O all my faith and all my love to tell her
That she will move from mourning into morning.

c. 1944   GEORGE BARKER

London, 1940

After fourteen hours clearing they came to him
Under the twisted girders and the rubble.
They would not let me see his face.
Now I sit shiftlessly on the tube platforms
Or huddle, a little tipsy, in brick-built shelters.
I can see with an indifferent eye
The red glare over by the docks and hear
Impassively the bomb-thuds in the distance.

For me, a man with not many interests
And no pretensions to fame, that was my world,
My son of fifteen, my only concrete achievement,
Whom they could not protect. Stepping aside
From the Great Crusade, I will play the idiot's part.
You, if you like, may wave your fists and crash
On the wrong doorsteps brash retaliation.

20 October 1940   FRANK THOMPSON
c. 1947

Ecce Homo

Whose is this horrifying face,
This putrid flesh, discoloured, flayed,
Fed on by flies, scorched by the sun?
Whose are these hollow red-filmed eyes
And thorn-spiked head and spear-stuck side?
Behold the Man: He is Man's Son.

Forget the legend, tear the decent veil
That cowardice or interest devised
To make their mortal enemy a friend,
To hide the bitter truth all His wounds tell,

Lest the great scandal be no more disguised:
He is in agony till the world's end,

And we must never sleep during that time!
He is suspended on the cross-tree now
And we are onlookers at the crime,
Callous contemporaries of the slow
Torture of God. Here is the hill
Made ghastly by His spattered blood

Whereon He hangs and suffers still:
See, the centurions wear riding-boots,
Black shirts and badges and peaked caps,
Greet one another with raised-arm salutes;
They have cold eyes, unsmiling lips;
Yet these His brothers know not what they do.

And on his either side hang dead
A labourer and a factory hand,
Or one is maybe a lynched Jew
And one a Negro or a Red,
Coolie or Ethiopian, Irishman,
Spaniard or German democrat.

Behind His lolling head the sky
Glares like a fiery cataract
Red with the murders of two thousand years
Committed in His name and by
Crusaders, Christian warriors
Defending faith and property.

Amid the plain beneath His transfixed hands,
Exuding darkness as indelible
As guilty stains, fanned by funereal
And lurid airs, besieged by drifting sands
And clefted landslides our about-to-be
Bombed and abandoned cities stand.

He who wept for Jerusalem
Now sees His prophecy extend
Across the greatest cities of the world,
A guilty panic reason cannot stem
Rising to raze them all as He foretold;
And He must watch this drama to the end.

Though often named, He is unknown
To the dark kingdoms at His feet
Where everything disparages His words,
And each man bears the common guilt alone
And goes blindfolded to his fate,
And fear and greed are sovereign lords.

The turning point of history
Must come. Yet the complacent and the proud
And who exploit and kill, may be denied –
Christ of Revolution and of Poetry –
The resurrection and the life
Wrought by your spirit's blood.

Involved in their own sophistry
The black priest and the upright man
Faced by subversive truth shall be struck dumb,
Christ of Revolution and of Poetry,
While the rejected and condemned become
Agents of the divine.

Not from a monstrance silver-wrought
But from the tree of human pain
Redeem our sterile misery,
Christ of Revolution and of Poetry,
That man's long journey through the night
May not have been in vain.

c. 1943   DAVID GASCOYNE

War Poet

I am the man who looked for peace and found
My own eyes barbed.
I am the man who groped for words and found
An arrow in my hand.
I am the builder whose firm walls surround
A slipping land.
When I grow sick or mad
Mock me not nor chain me:
When I reach for the wind
Cast me not down:
Though my face is a burnt book
And a wasted town.

March 1942   SIDNEY KEYES
c. 1945

A Soldier, Dying of Wounds, Speaks to Me on May 9th, 1945

You will remain. Do not hope much
From the husks of heavy archives:
Their tongues bark dusty lies that touch
Your footway. The enemy has lives
Still and a long language. You will clutch
Many times there, and you will flicker
Like a lamp in the wind. Your mark
Is known, for it does not beat quicker
Than an old cradle. Search the dark
For signs, and the far light
For footprints from the night.

102

Do not dream much in the waiting years,
Nor guess an incredible way
Up mountain clouds or down damp stairs
Through the illiterate dark. Each day
The ambush is armed against your heirs,
Levies are laid on living and dying.
I am among those who have died;
All our deaths, like a hurt child crying,
Are only a by-work. The wind-tide,
Water-call, fall of rain,
Are for those who remain.

c. 1950   DORIAN COOKE

The Middle of a War

My photograph already looks historic.
The promising youthful face, the matelot's collar,
Say 'This one is remembered for a lyric.
His place and period – nothing could be duller.'

Its position is already indicated –
The son or brother in the album; pained
The expression and the garments dated,
His fate so obviously preordained.

The original turns away; as horrible thoughts,
Loud fluttering aircraft slope above his head
At dusk. The ridiculous empires break like biscuits.
Ah, life has been abandoned by the boats –
Only the trodden island and the dead
Remain, and the once inestimable caskets.

c. 1942   ROY FULLER

Soldiers Bathing

The sea at evening moves across the sand.
Under a reddening sky I watch the freedom of a band
Of soldiers who belong to me. Stripped bare
For bathing in the sea, they shout and run in the warm
  air;
Their flesh worn by the trade of war, revives
And my mind towards the meaning of it strives.

All's pathos now. The body that was gross,
Rank, ravenous, disgusting in the act or in repose,
All fever, filth and sweat, its bestial strength
And bestial decay, by pain and labour grows at length
Fragile and luminous. 'Poor bare forked animal,'
Conscious of his desires and needs and flesh that rise and
  fall,
Stands in the soft air, tasting after toil
The sweetness of his nakedness: letting the sea-waves coil
Their frothy tongues about his feet, forgets
His hatred of the war, its terrible pressure that begets
A machinery of death and slavery,
Each being a slave and making slaves of others: finds that he
Remembers his old freedom in a game
Mocking himself, and comically mimics fear and shame.

He plays with death and animality;
And reading in the shadows of his pallid flesh, I see
The idea of Michelangelo's cartoon
Of soldiers bathing, breaking off before they were half
  done
At some sortie of the enemy, an episode
Of the Pisan wars with Florence. I remember how he
  showed

Their muscular limbs that clamber from the water,
And heads that turn across the shoulder, eager for the
  slaughter,
Forgetful of their bodies that are bare,
And hot to buckle on and use the weapons lying there.
– And I think too of the theme another found
When, shadowing men's bodies on a sinister red ground,
Another Florentine, Pollaiuolo,
Painted a naked battle: warriors, straddled, hacked the
  foe,
Dug their bare toes into the ground and slew
The brother-naked man who lay between their feet and
  drew
His lips back from his teeth in a grimace.

They were Italians who knew war's sorrow and disgrace
And showed the thing suspended, stripped: a theme
Born out of the experience of war's horrible extreme
Beneath a sky where even the air flows
With lacrimae Christi. For that rage, that bitterness, those
  blows,
That hatred of the slain, what could they be
But indirectly or directly a commentary
On the Crucifixion? And the picture burns
With indignation and pity and despair by turns,
Because it is the obverse of the scene
Where Christ hangs murdered, stripped, upon the Cross.
  I mean,
That is the explanation of its rage.

And we too have our bitterness and pity that engage
Blood, spirit, in this war. But night begins,
Night of the mind: who nowadays is conscious of our
  sins?
Though every human deed concerns our blood,

And even we must know, what nobody has understood,
That some great love is over all we do,
And that is what has driven us to this fury, for so few
Can suffer all the terror of that love:
The terror of that love has set us spinning in this groove
Greased with our blood.

                  These dry themselves and dress,
Combing their hair, forget the fear and shame of
   nakedness.
Because to love is frightening we prefer
The freedom of our crimes. Yet, as I drink the dusky air,
I feel a strange delight that fills me full,
Strange gratitude, as if evil itself were beautiful,
And kiss the wound in thought, while in the west
I watch a streak of red that might have issued from Christ's
   breast.

1942
c. 1954

                                      F. T. PRINCE

Ultima Thule

I can see him now, the homesick Roman soldier,
– All Britain creeping up behind his back
Like a wild beast – standing upon Cape Wrath
Staring into the north, across the sea,
Into the mist, the amorphous coiling white,
A conquered world behind him and there ahead
Nothing but sea and wet mist salt on the tongue
Almost like blood. And suddenly it lifts.
There surely far far to the north – an island?

I know that terror squeezes him like a sponge,
I know that he turns and desperately calls

'Come quickly quickly come, do you see it, see it,
There, an island there? The end of the world.'
They come half running up the desolate cape,
(Quick now before the mist enfolds the vision)
'We have seen the end of the world.'

We have seen the end of the world.
And I have stood
On the cliff above Dover, staring into the south
Upon the edge of the world no less than he.
Southward the mist is thick and it is easy
To think there is nothing there, nothing at all
Save the quaking sea for ever, and mist for ever.

But I know what is there.
I need no one to tell me what to see.
Yet if I called to the little boy who is playing
Up by the sheepfold and asked him: 'What do you see?'
He'd say: 'The sea, the mist. What do you see?'
'The beginning of the world.' And he perhaps,
'What do you mean by that?' Then could I tell him?

c. 1946   PATRIC DICKINSON

Lying Awake

Lying awake, he'll watch the moonlight alter
The shape of dune and hollow; like a hound
Light rounds its herd of shadows to the water
Whose shoring silver is the only sound:
But no wind stirs below the racing stars
That, where the heavens roll their bitter blue,
Sail the cloud-isles and archipelagos
Of burning frost, snowed fire, and fiery snow.

Through the tent entrance parted back like hair
The moonlight limes their presence in slow paths,
Falls upon book and pipe and photographs,
Candle and bottle and the things they wear,
Impartially as on old bones out there
Bleaching beyond the sandhill cenotaphs.

Sleep is the antidote against the night.
The others sleep; and in their husks of flesh
Hold the sweet kernel of a quiet mind.
He only wakes; and through his brain, like sand,
The scorpion of fear, the snake of doubt,
Crawl with their venom, lacerate and lash
The hand grown senseless and the eyes gone blind.

More than the night airs bless the sleeping limbs
Of those who need not seek love's substitutes:
Hands in the dark at home caress the place
Those limbs lay once in tangible embrace,
And through half-sentient finger-tips there shoots
Remembrance distance fosters as it dims.

These in the daily letter to the lover,
Or from the lover, keep the roots of life
Alive within them; only half-discover
The grey hair and the fatigable breath.
For them the slow parabola of days
Climbs up to arcs of known futurities.
But from his phoenix hour the days go down
Into the dark ways of oblivion.

Lying awake, he'll watch the moon, and drown.

c. 1946   JAMES WALKER

Survivors

With the ship burning in their eyes
The white faces float like refuse
In the darkness – the water screwing
Oily circles where the hot steel lies.

They clutch with fingers frozen into claws
The lifebelts thrown from a destroyer,
And see, between the future's doors,
The gasping entrance of the sea.

Taken on board as many as lived, who
Had a mind left for living and the ocean,
They open eyes running with surf,
Heavy with the grey ghosts of explosion.

The meaning is not yet clear,
Where daybreak died in the smile –
And the mouth remained stiff
And grinning, stupid for a while.

But soon they joke, easy and warm,
As men will who have died once
Yet somehow were able to find their way –
Muttering this was not included in their pay.

Later, sleepless at night, the brain spinning
With cracked images, they won't forget
The confusion and the oily dead,
Nor yet the casual knack of living.

p. 1942   ALAN ROSS

Goodbye

So we must say Goodbye, my darling,
and go, as lovers go, for ever;
Tonight remains, to pack and fix on labels
And make an end of lying down together.

I put a final shilling in the gas,
And watch you slip your dress below your knees
And lie so still I hear your rustling comb
Modulate the autumn in the trees.

And all the countless things I shall remember
Lay mummy-cloths of silence round my head;
I fill the carafe with a drink of water;
You say 'We paid a guinea for this bed,'

And then, 'We'll leave some gas, a little warmth
For the next resident, and these dry flowers,'
And turn your face away, afraid to speak
The big word, that Eternity is ours.

Your kisses close my eyes and yet you stare
As though God struck a child with nameless fears;
Perhaps the water glitters and discloses
Time's chalice and its limpid useless tears.

Everything we renounce except our selves;
Selfishness is the last of all to go;
Our sighs are exhalations of the earth,
Our footprints leave a track across the snow.

We made the universe to be our home,
Our nostrils took the wind to be our breath,

Our hearts are massive towers of delight,
We stride across the seven seas of death.

Yet when all's done you'll keep the emerald
I placed upon your finger in the street;
And I will keep the patches that you sewed
On my old battledress tonight, my sweet.

c. 1945   ALUN LEWIS

Stand-to

The sea at dawn is grey, sombre as metal,
With dull unburnished strength
The light expands till the horizon,
Once more defined, encircles our day.
In the tufted grass and the sea-pinks
Our rifles lie, clean, with bolts oiled,
Our pouches hard with rounds.
A metal world of rifle, sea and sky.

The cramped limb moves; the eyes stare outwards.
Only behind is life where the fields stretch
And new smoke lifts from silent houses.

We forget the pre-vigil days
The time of fretting and proposition
Of clamorous words and fear be-devilled plans.
Perhaps we were wrong then,
And all the holy words
Were cried in a madman's dream:
Peace and freedom
Dwelled in the clarity of delirium;

The scales of justice balanced neatly
Not now, but in the future of a mirage.

We have returned to faith
For the argument did not reach its conclusion.
The words were buried by bullets, and the guns
   drowned our songs.
Here, leaning on the side of the weapon-pit,
A trickle of sand on our boots
There is only the tense eye and the tired mind
That does not plead or suffer but has learned patience.

p. 1942   NEIL MCCALLUM

Bivouac

There was no trace of Heaven
That night as we lay
Punch-drunk and blistered with sunlight
On the ploughed-up clay.

I remembered the cactus where our wheels
Had bruised it, bleeding white;
And a fat rat crouching beadyeyed
Caught by my light;

And the dry disturbing whispers
Of the agitated wood,
With its leathery vendetta,
Mantillas dark with blood.

And the darkness drenched with Evil
Haunting as a country song,
Ignoring the protesting cry
Of Right and of Wrong.

Yet the peasant was drawing water
With the first excited bird
And the dawn with childish eyes
Observed us as we stirred

And the milk-white oxen waited
Docile at the yoke
As we clipped on our equipment
And scarcely spoke

Being bewildered by the night
And only aware
Of the withering obsession
That lovers grow to fear
When the last note is written
And at last and alone
One of them wakes in terror
And the other is gone.

c. 1945   ALUN LEWIS

Day's Journey

Starting at early light from the old fort
Across the dry flaked mud, you remember,
We left the well on our right and the crosses,
Drove west all day through the camel-scrub,
Tossing in convoy like a mobile orchard,
An olive-yard on wheels, irregular,
Spaced over miles : were bombed : were bombed again,
Until the air was dust : drove on due west
Past the sheikh's tomb of stones, past the dry spring,
Until at dusk from the escarpment
Rumbled and boomed the gun's resentment,

Impersonal, the protest of a Titan
Impartially disgusted, while the sun
Signed off in angry flames.
                              We halted,
Quietly, in close leaguer, half ashamed.

15 December 1941   FRANK THOMPSON
c. 1947

Battalion H. Q., Burma

Dante imagined it thus, and Dore reading
Saw eye to eye with him. The signallers crouch
In their dark holes tense as the wires that reach
For the tilted pole. Watch the torsos swing
In the hot pit as the dust peels like petals
Of thin ruin from the cliff face, and when
The guns shout in the narrow valleys, a little
More shifts, like a girl arranging her dress,
At the start of the party waiting for the young men.

There in the black tunnels, like red blood
The lines hang from the telephones, and the heat
Grins, palpable, commanding, like a foreman stood
Astride his ditches. See where the colonel sits
In his Dante-cum-Dore inferno, apart,
Gesturing like a fastidious actor, correct
And cool with his veined hands.
                              A small part,
No lifting of heavy words to the gilded darkness,
But charming, and in a quiet way, almost perfect.

p. 1945   IVOR ROBERTS-JONES

Tunisian Patrol

The Night lies with her body crookedly flung
In agony across the sharp hills;
By the fitful moon her nostrils are taut, quivering;
She is tensed in cold sweat and lonely fear,
Giving sudden birth in dark, sly, trodden places
To her unlawful issue, blind, hideous Death.

Across the pain-jerked body of the Night
We must go, taking the new-born Death in arms,
Holding it close, warmly to us, as our own,
Giving it new games to play, new toys to tear apart.

c. 1944   RICHARD SPENDER

Dunkirk Pier

Deeply across the waves of our darkness fear,
like the silent octopus, feeling, groping, clear
as a star's reflection, nervous and cold as a bird,
tells us that pain, tells us that death is near.

Why should a woman telling above her fire
incantations of evening, thoughts that are
older and paler than history, why should this lark
exploring extinction and oneness of self and air

remind us that, lonely and lost as flowers in deserted
weed-mastered gardens, each faint face averted
from the inescapable confusion, for each of us slowly
death on his last, most hideous journey has started?

What was our sin? – that heartless to the end
falls now the heavy sickle on foe, on friend,
and those that we love, value and regret
surrender quickest to death's empty hand.

Failure to suffer? We who in years past
have suffered, yes, in this or that, but in the last
irrevocable act of suffering, as a dog suffers deeply,
blindly, completely, are not versed.

What hope for the future? Can we who see the tide
ebbing along the shore, the greedy, lined
with shadows, dare with puny words support
a future which belongs to others? Dare we bind

now, at this last moment of sunshine above
the crests of oncoming events, like waves which move
remorselessly nearer, future generations
with sacrifice? We who taught hate, expect them to love?

c. 1942   ALAN ROOK

Simplify Me When I'm Dead

Remember me when I am dead
and simplify me when I'm dead.

As the processes of earth
strip off the colour and the skin:
take the brown hair and blue eye

and leave me simpler than at birth,
when hairless I came howling in
as the moon entered the cold sky.

Of my skeleton perhaps,
so stripped, a learned man will say
'He was of such a type and intelligence,' no more.

Thus when in a year collapse
particular memories, you may
deduce, from the long pain I bore

the opinions I held, who was my foe
and what I left, even my appearance
but incidents will be no guide.

Time's wrong-way telescope will show
a minute man ten years hence
and by distance simplified.

Through that lens see if I seem
substance or nothing: of the world
deserving mention or charitable oblivion,

not by momentary spleen
or love into decision hurled,
leisurely arrived at an opinion.

Remember me when I am dead
and simplify me when I'm dead.

c. 1951   KEITH DOUGLAS

The Album

Arab, American and German
dead beneath a Gascon vine –
are they not a madman's scribbled
chaos that he called design?

In the album's ordered pages
were, no less for each of these
than for moth or stamp or photo,
documented categories –

did he think, poor crazed collector,
removing separative pins,
confusing all, that here was order
new made among his specimens?

Or was it weariness, not madness –
was it the grey, the jaded curse
of one grown sick as of a surfeit,
sick of his album-universe?

October 1944   JAMES MONAHAN
c. 1948

Europe's Prisoners

Never a day, never a day passes
But I remember them, their stoneblind faces
Beaten by arclights, their eyes turned inward
Seeking an answer and their passage homeward:

For being citizens of time, they never
Would learn the body's nationality.
Tortured for years now, they refuse to sever
Spirit from flesh or accept our callow century.

Not without hope, but lacking present solace,
The preacher knows the feel of nails and grace;
The singer snores; the orator's facile hands
Are fixed in a gesture no one understands.

Others escaped, yet paid for their betrayal:
Even the politicians with their stale
Visions and cheap flirtation with the past
Will not die any easier at the last.

The ones who took to garrets and consumption
In foreign cities, found a deeper dungeon
Than any Dachau. Free but still confined
The human lack of pity split their mind.

Whatever days, whatever seasons pass,
The prisoners must stare in pain's white face:
Until at last the courage they have learned
Shall burst the walls and overturn the world.

21 May 1941   SIDNEY KEYES
c. 1945

Seventh Elegy

April 1943

But now they rise and push us from our stools . . .

I saw the dead flocking the Strand today.
The trees whose floral tributes fill the gardens
are ordered by their allies underground –
horrible blossom, which unmarried fingers
prepare, like children's clothes, against their coming.

We must confine them – they have broken out –
the fields are broken, the cold glass of the ground,
the bars of the hills, the frontier of the sea.
Out of the prison never in history
opened before, out of the valleys, voiceless but rebels. . . .

For the barriers become blurred. The skin of the soil
has risen over our heads. Invisible trees
spread quiet roots among our roads and houses.
This is the earth that covers us, like a sea,
a wind whose birds are stones, whose clouds are trees.

We must confine them – they have broken out –
now whitest faces shine at every table.
The living are hollow, and the speechless dead
break the unmarried night of the sea – invaders
with faces we know among us. We are betrayed.

For mother this is not the son you bore
nor this your lover, daughter – hollow skins
forfeit and smiling sit the table round:
London lies buried under a dune of sky –
a mile above us wave the summer's crops –

I know them by the coldness of their hands.

c. 1944   ALEX COMFORT

The End of Love

Now he is dead
How should I know
My true love's arms
From wind and snow?

No man I meet
In field or house,
Though in the street
A hundred pass.

The hurrying dust
Has never a face,
No longer human
In man or woman.

Now he is gone
Why should I mourn
My true love more
Than mud or stone?

c. 1949　KATHLEEN RAINE

Perspective

To walk back into love,
Into that summer garden where the heart
Opened as flowers . . .

*

Eyes in the dead of night
Waking from sleep will stare and slowly search
Their lost surroundings,

Knobs, table, washstand
Outlined adrift in darkness; no direction,
No known perspective,

Till sense of place returns,
Window and doorway the familiar marks
Taking alignment.

To wake back into love
Would be as dubious and as bewildered,
As known and certain.

p. 1945　　　　　　　PAUL WIDDOWS

Hereafter

How shall men turn their minds again to peace
who live by violence in these years of war
and make of hate an honour for desire:
how shall they after all be gentle
who all hours are forbidden to be kind?

I see the sorrow of the men of death
walking the narrow road in the silent sun:
the murdered woman with the shattered head,
the child that never hated smashed by hate;
the bitter faction of the broken bottle
and the razor battle in our common street.

O once the germ has coursed the blood
along the tunnel of the vein
and in the chamber of the brain
gathered its garrison and built its fort
no politic or proclamation
or dispensation of a Janus church
can drive the madness out or mend the soul.

c. 1945   SEAN JENNET

During a Bombardment by V-Weapons

The little noises of the house:
Drippings between the slates and ceiling;
From the electric fire's cooling
Tickings; the dry feet of a mouse:

These at the ending of a war
Have power to alarm me more
Than the ridiculous detonations
Outside the gently coughing curtains.

And, love, I see your pallor bears
A far more pointed threat than steel.
Now all the permanent and real
Furies are settling in upstairs.

1945   ROY FULLER
c. 1949

War

Cold are the stones
That built the wall of Troy,
Cold are the bones
Of the dead Greek boy

Who for some vague thought
Of honour fell,
Nor why he fought
Could clearly tell.

Innocence hired to kill
Lies pitilessly dead.
Stone and bone lie still.
Helen turns in bed.

c. 1946   PATRIC DICKINSON

Armistice

It is finished. The enormous dust-cloud over Europe
Lifts like a million swallows; and a light,
Drifting in craters, touches the quiet dead.

Now, at the bugle's hour, before the blood
Cakes in a clean wind on their marble faces,
Making them monuments; before the sun,

Hung like a medal on the smoky noon,
Whitens the bone that feeds the earth; before
Wheat-ear springs green, again, in the green spring

And they are bread in the bodies of the young:
Be strong to remember how the bread died, screaming;
Gangrene was corn, and monuments went mad.

c. 1949   PAUL DEHN

Poem on Returning Home from the Wars After Six Years' Absence

What would be best
Of the remembered of living or dead
To call from multiple-wounded, hidden places?
Or the high after-crest
Of an earthquake may suddenly spread
More masonry on skulls and living faces.

Not of my choice
Are the shapes that ride on visible sound,

– My seven loud brothers buried overseas,
The warm, green, gentle voice
Of my seven sisters underground,
And music tangled in the roots of trees.

Somewhere I dare
To scour uprooted woods and scratch my hands
Among the war-picked ruins that still mark
These towns, to tease and tear
Thick scabs from unremembered lands
And smash the stone slabs that shut out the dark.

It would be best
Of the forgotten of the dark and light
To make a peculiar identity;
And from the locked, deep chest
Of the forbidden of sound and sight
To excavate its guardian enemy.

Who could forget
The pain gained in the lost years, in the waste
Times between killing and dying? This pain
Remains and moves to fret
The coupled strings of touch and taste
And prick the coloured bubbles of the brain.

Again, to make
Of warring fissions one identity
Is a kind of destruction – as the waves
Of an explosion break
Sound, flesh, and stone, and the shocked sky
Shakes with the emptying of its guarded graves.

And of the last
Who have remained are those who are worn strange,

Who watch, without welcome or grief, a cold
Room in a hanging past
(As in a mirror blind to change)
With their own living and dead and the unknown old.

There we who are
The exact last comers of the first gone
Are seen only as shapes that file and fall
Between the near and far
Dead, or sit with the living like iron
Shadows between the window and the wall.

Who now remembers
Of the last or first of numberless dead
The new ways or the old ways? And who will dare
To walk back six Decembers
And dig the mud of that dark bed
To the roots of these Summer wounds we bear?

They all go down,
Drowned in their visions, who would live again
Across these ruined landscapes where huge seas
From some still-standing town
Have swept the ground of grass and grain,
Have lopped the limbs and bent the trunks of trees.

So there is still
The inevitable answer: there is no
Time to return along the loaded days
That lead under the hill
Where wind and blood and water flow
Into the vortex of an endless maze.

Somewhere I must
Unmake the shadow substance of these hosts

Whose hands beyond the shut-out dark invade
Like magnets in the dust.
Their world ends; and all its masks and ghosts
Must crumble as the separate visions fade.

c. 1950   DORIAN COOKE

A Warning to Politicians

The bells proclaim the immediate joy,
The horror and the killing cease;
They drag within the walls of Troy
The wooden horse of Peace.

c. 1946   PATRIC DICKINSON

'THE TRAVELLER HAS REGRETS...'

The Traveller Has Regrets

The traveller has regrets
For the receding shore
That with its many nets
Has caught, not to restore,
The white lights in the bay,
The blue lights on the hill,
Though night with many stars
May travel with him still,
But night has nought to say,
Only a colour and shape
Changing like cloth shaking,
A dancer with a cape
Whose dance is heart-breaking,
Night with its many stars
Can warn travellers
There's only time to kill
And nothing much to say:
But the blue lights on the hill,
The white lights in the bay
Told us the meal was laid
And that the bed was made
And that we could not stay.

1942   G. S. FRASER
c. 1948

Spring Letter

The earth turns over, our side feels the cold . . .

Lovely, but here no part of me, the world
rolls under shadow like a woollen ball:
all terror's darkening magazine, the cold
indecency of outward violence, will
grown lecherous with death, all crouching might
of iron, being far, even seems beautiful.

The wind's cold surplice in the sky, I sit
here, in the washed and choirboy afternoon;
and the grass claps its coloured fingers at
the clarity of water; and the sun
is in my hair like a chrysanthemum.
For here the will of quietness is done.

No, not of war: the dragon and the drum
that pulse his blood about the world are here
a breast beneath my hand, and out of time.
This tall season is my chanteclere
from night in mirrors, cannon flowering
like falling trees; all ceremony of war.

Calm acres and Mozartean air, spring
with its cold confetti in the boughs,
are not the world but a more inward thing:
as a wet garment on the body shows
the curl of limb and muscle, this day
droops in the shape of secret images.

Love, and the lovely clothing of its play,
its thinking film upon the flesh; the stride
and ache of afterthought to our long woe

our tenderness, the hangman of the blood:
here in your flowered scarf of Egypt, deep
as seasons under water, blooms our good.

A silkwhite skein of egrets that sew-up
the ploughman's gashes on a field: our words
have glittered so across a wounded hope
and been a splendid prophecy of birds;
and the wet crops that flourish towards sand
in growing wildfire, the childbed of seeds,

are in the planets' march to us, our end.
Oh infinite progression from our close-
cupped origin, acorn of stellar wind!
Here in the olive-shadows of our peace
is movement too intense for motion, heart
of a great tigerish whirlwind over us.

More terrible than fear, that bestial heat
rages beyond our vision and is safe:
iron insects with locked horns, the beat
of heavy air, horrible cells of life
that is not man but built of him, the smash
of wings and bodies; anger, dismay, grief:

all pain that makes a bugle of the flesh
turn there to awful beauty, beautiful
because our lives are under it. This hush
we know our love by, and our secret will,
is the exceeding clamour of the bat.
Then here I see our union grow full,

the wind's old scars and wounds cut into it,
a strip of hazel-shining foil, the river.
Fast in the river's darkening mind, I sit

and reach towards Europe, pitiful as a lover
through this enormous shadow of the world,
while beautiful and remote, the world turns over.

Near Madi, 1942   TERENCE TILLER
c. 1947

Egyptian Dancer

Slowly, with intention to tempt, she sidles out
    (a smile and a shake of bells)
in silver, tight as a fish's, and a web
of thin-flame veils, and her brown buttery flesh
(but she is a mermaid with twelve metal tails)
    glimpsed or guessed by seconds.

Slowly the insidious unison sucks her in,
    and the rhythm of the drums,
the mournful feline quavering whose pulse
runs through her limbs; shivering like a bride
she lifts her arms into a lyre; there comes
    a sense of nakedness

as the red gauze floats off; and of release.
    She is all silver-finned:
it hangs from wrist and ankle, she is silver-
feather-crowned, tight silver across the breasts;
skirt of bright strips; and where in the fat forced up
    her navel winks like a wound.

The dance begins: she ripples like a curtain;
    her arms are snakes
– she is all serpent, she coils on her own loins

134

and shakes the bells; her very breasts are alive
and writhing, and around the emphatic sex
        her thighs are gimlets of oil.

All the half-naked body, as if tortured
        or loving with a ghost,
labours; the arms are lifted to set free
atrocious lust or anguish, and the worms
that are fingers crack as croupe or bust
        or belly rolls to the drums.

Wilder: the drift of the sand-spout the wavering
        curve of the legs grow a blaze
and a storm while the obsession of music hammers
  and wails
to her dim eyes to her shrieking desire of the flesh
that is dumb with an ecstasy of movement and plays
        fiercely the squirming act

and sweat breaks out she is bright as metal while
  the skirt
        spins like a flower at her hips
into the last unbearable glorious agony
between the lips and suddenly, it is over:
a last groan of the drum, panting she drops
        into the darkness of past love.

c. 1943   TERENCE TILLER

Behaviour of Fish in an
Egyptian Tea Garden

As a white stone draws down the fish
she on the seafloor of the afternoon
draws down men's glances and their cruel wish
for love. Slyly red lip on the spoon

slips in a morsel of ice-cream; her hands
white as a milky stone, white submarine
fronds, sink with spread fingers, lean
along the table, carmined at the ends.

A cotton magnate, an important fish
with great eyepouches and a golden mouth
through the frail reefs of furniture swims out
and idling, suspended, stays to watch.

A crustacean old man clamped to his chair
sits coldly near her and might see
her charms through fissures where the eyes should be
or else his teeth are parted in a stare.

Captain on leave, a lean dark mackerel,
lies in the offing; turns himself and looks
through currents of sound. The flat-eyed flatfish sucks
on a straw, staring from its repose, laxly.

And gallants in shoals swim up and lag,
circling and passing near the white attraction;
sometimes pausing, opening a conversation;
fish pause so to nibble or tug.

Now the ice-cream is finished, is
paid for. The fish swim off on business

and she sits alone at the table, a white stone
useless except to a collector, a rich man.

Cairo, 8 October 1943   KEITH DOUGLAS
c. 1951

Egypt

Who knows the lights at last, who knows the cities
And the unloving hands upon the thighs
Would yet return to seek his home-town pretties
For the shy finger-tips and sidelong eyes.

Who knows the world, the flesh, the compromises
Would go back to the theory in the book:
Who knows the place the poster advertises
Back to the poster for another look.

But nets the fellah spreads beside the river
Where the green waters criss-cross in the sun
End certain migratory hopes for ever:
In that white light, all shadows are undone.

The desert slays. But safe from Allah's justice
Where the broad river of His Mercy lies,
Where ground for labour, or where scope for lust is,
The crooked and tall and cunning cities rise.

The green Nile irrigates a barren region,
All the coarse palms are ankle-deep in sand;
No love roots deep, though easy loves are legion:
The heart's as hot and hungry as the hand.

In airless evenings, at the café table,
The soldier sips his thick sweet coffee up:
The dry grounds, like the moral to my fable,
Are bitter at the bottom of the cup.

p. 1946   G. S. FRASER

Effort

Here I sit and sweat all day;
Here I sweat to earn my pay;
Four rupees a day I get
To sit and sit, and sweat and sweat.

p. 1945   REG LEVY

Dead Sea Plage

Where once Lot's wife looked back in horror
To see God's judgment blast Gomorrah
To-day the Sodom sunshine blisters
Queen Alexandra's Nursing Sisters.

p. 1945   ROBERT LIDDELL

Cairo Jag

Shall I get drunk or cut myself a piece of cake,
a pasty Syrian with a few words of English
or the Turk who says she is a princess – she dances
apparently by levitation? Or Marcelle, Parisienne
always preoccupied with her dull dead lover:
she has all the photographs and his letters
tied in a bundle and stamped *Décédé* in mauve ink.
All this takes place in a stink of jasmin.

But there are the streets dedicated to sleep
stenches and sour smells, the sour cries
do not disturb their application to slumber
all day, scattered on the pavement like rags
afflicted with fatalism and hashish. The women
offering their children brown-paper breasts
dry and twisted, elongated like the skull,
Holbein's signature. But this stained white town
is something in accordance with mundane conventions –
Marcelle drops her Gallic airs and tragedy
suddenly shrieks in Arabic about the fare
with the cabman, links herself so
with the somnambulists and legless beggars:
it is all one, all as you have heard.

But by a day's travelling you reach a new world
the vegetation is of iron
dead tanks, gun barrels split like celery
the metal brambles have no flowers or berries
and there are all sorts of manure, you can imagine
the dead themselves, their boots, clothes and possessions
clinging to the ground, a man with no head
has a packet of chocolate and a souvenir of Tripoli.

p. 1945   KEITH DOUGLAS

Desert

Hereabouts is desert, it's a bad country,
grows nothing, nothing to show for, sand has no
   whereabouts,
goes everywhere and nowhere like a sea:
yes, I said, and noticed the flash of sun on grit
and knew that all the hourglasses in the world had broken
and this was the sum of all the hours of the world.

Did you ever see a man bleed in sand? I
asked him, did you ever see a soldier, a khaki
hero with his life blood blotting entirely and quickly
into the khaki sand? Did you ever see a man drown in
   quicksand
or, let alone a man, a tree or a bedstead?

It's not just that there's so much of it, he said,
nor the bitter heat of it nor its blinding glare
but it's the shiftlessness, that there's no purpose here,
nothing but a blanket warming a blanket, or a sum
multiplying and dividing itself forever, a sum
adding and subtracting itself for ever and ever.

c. 1945   PATRICK ANDERSON

Ring Plover at El Alamein

Nothing grows on the sand-flats
Beside the salt lake at El Alamein,
The water is still and rust-pink,
And the flat sand rim is crusted with salt.

Beyond the white dunes and the shallow beach
Is the brilliant tideless sea;
Behind is the endless sand.

Yet here at the dead lake's side
I saw a solitary ring plover –
Small and plump and coloured,
Black and white and red,
Surprising as a painted wooden toy.
He and I alone had the pale shore,
I still and watching him,
The bird busy as an absorbed small boy:
He ran importantly, bobbed and cocked his head,
Small and pre-occupied, always hurrying,
As if he were always a little behind.
So I have seen him on busy beaches of the North
Hunting with the dunlin, between the fishing-boats
And the nets hung on poles to dry
Along the shores of the Moray Firth.

But like memory the quick wings flickered,
Left momentarily a white arc in the air,
And he was over the dunes, out to sea.
I was alone on the sand-flats
Beside the rust-pink water.

October–November 1942   JOHN JARMAIN
p. 1946

Burial Flags, Sind

Here with the desert so austere that only
Flags live, plant out your flags upon the wind,
Red tattered bannerets that mark a lonely
    Grave in the sand;

A crude oblong of stone to guard some mortal
Remains against a jackal's rooting paws
Painted with colour-wash to look like marble
    Through the heat-haze;

Roofed casually with corrugated iron
Held up by jutting and uneven poles;
The crooked flagpoles tied to a curved headstone
    Carved with symbols –

Stars and new moon that are the only flowers
To grow out of this naked earth and sky,
Except these flags that through the windy hours
    Bloom steadily,

Dull red, the faded red of women's garments
Carried on sudden camels past the sky –
Red strips of cloth that ride the dusty heavens
    Untiringly.

p. 1945   R. N. CURREY

Monsoon

Clouds rise like white steam from the cooler hills
And rain along their flanks is drink of Tantalus
To the miserable plain. Cumulus mounts and swells
Proudly, then mumbling melts and drifts away
Impotently, adding its moisture to the brimming air.

My flesh is rotten, spongy, and my skin
Is cobbled with sweatdrops, scraped with the shaly rash
Of prickly heat; and all my being within
(Its taut strings slacked by dampness, frayed by men)
Has no more power for motion than the sullen air.

Night brings no ease. Even the brightest stars
Glimmer like sad sea-pearls behind the mist,
And lesser lights are stifled. No wind stirs
The thick damp felt of darkness. Insects' hum
Is the far dynamo that electrifies the air.

O God, send rain, rain.
Summon the mighty ocean, mount on a swift wind
The waters of the wide bay, fling them against the sun's
Fierce throne in cataracts, bring up the guns
Of thunder to smash it in tumbling towers of sound.

Let this world cease
In a cool deluge drowning consciousness;
Cover me, Lord, with the lovely oblivion of rain.

p. 1945   K. R. GRAY

An Undistinguished Coast

The long flow of time about him
Works like water, steadily
Carves the littoral of feature;
Those who know him well,
Like fishermen a coast familiar,
Note change in banks and shoals that move,
In every gesture the action of the tides.
The first storm, years ago, did damage,
Blocked the channels, undermined a lip,
And equinoctial gales have left a stammer.
Where the salt current nags the shore,
The rocks are frayed, the glance unfocused;
The slipping tide licks at a razor edge
And the whole beach is raw;
There are things he dare not think of.
In the still creek the oil that kills the gulls
Thickens on rotting baulks
And water in the deep holes
Whorls the limestone: underneath the eyes
The pouches grow; and the bright fish have gone.
You need no chart to read this story;
Forty years are written here,
A common undistinguished shore.

p. 1946   ROBIN FEDDEN

This Unimportant Morning

This unimportant morning
Something goes singing where
The capes turn over on their sides
And the warm Adriatic rides
Her blue and sun washing
At the edge of the world and its brilliant cliffs.

Day rings in the higher airs
Pure with cicadas and slowing
Like a pulse to smoke from farms,
Extinguished in the exhausted earth,
Unclenching like a fist and going.

Trees, fume, cool, pour – and overflowing
Unstretch the feathers of birds and shake
Carpets in windows, brush with dew
The up-and-doing, and young lovers now
Their little resurrections make.

And now lightly to kiss all whom sleep
Stitched up – and wake, my darling, wake;
The impatient Boatman has been waiting
Under the house, his long oars folded up
Like wings in waiting on the darkling lake.

p. 1945   LAWRENCE DURRELL

On the Road

Our roof was grapes, and the broad hands of the vine
as we two drank in the vine-chinky shade
of harvest France:
and wherever the white road led we could not care;
it had brought us there
to the arbour built on a valley side where Time,
if Time any more existed, was that river
of so profound a current, it at once
both flowed and stayed.

We two. And nothing in the whole world was lacking.
It is later one realizes. I forget
the exact year or what we said. But the place
for a lifetime glows with noon; there are the rustic
table and the benches set; across the river
forests as soft as fallen clouds; and in
our wine and eyes I remember other noons.
It is a lot to say, nothing was lacking.
River, sun and leaves; and I am making
words to say 'grapes' and 'her skin'.

p. 1947   BERNARD SPENCER

Tananarive

Hills blossom in small red houses: the Palace
Governs like an implacable queen her plains
And lazing people. The children play like ducklings.
All are so happy but nothing here seems clean
Except the gull-like washing and white arum lilies.

146

We take over the bars and speak English arrogantly,
Stare at the pigeon-crouching French whose faces
Speak with their voices. Rhum, citron and orange pressé:
And sly, beautiful soignée women take
No notice at all of our caps and Sam Brownes.

Flags are saluted everywhere: above the dusty street
High in the lilac trees we see from the verandah
The ice-like stillness of encircling ricefields, greenly
    glinting;
Pousse-pousse boys jolt past like broken toys
And above us all the time frowns the forbidding palace.

Some of it is quite lovely. Down in the market place
An acre of red and white carnations, a moving scent of
    cloves,
And girls like Hedy dressed in Gauguin colours
Slipping among the striding, pavement-singing soldiers.
And subtle, ageless children more wicked than any pirate.

Till night holds all its treacheries cupped like a black
    breast
With light in the town its sensuous, desirous smile.
All over the small hills depart the ambushing steps
That crumble and snare; and in the drifting gloom
The velvet stab of pleasure that pushes to the heart.

September 1942   BERNARD GUTTERIDGE
p. 1944

The Giraffes

I think before they saw me the giraffes
Were watching me. Over the golden grass,
The bush and ragged open tree of thorn,
From a grotesque height, under their lightish horns,
Their eyes were fixed on mine as I approached them.
The hills behind descended steeply: iron
Coloured outcroppings of rock half covered by
Dull green and sepia vegetation, dry
And sunlit: and above, the piercing blue
Where clouds like islands lay or like swans flew.

Seen from those hills the scrubby plain is like
A large-scale map whose features have a look
Half menacing, half familiar, and across
Its brightness arms of shadow ceaselessly
Revolve. Like small forked twigs or insects move
Giraffes, upon the great map where they live.

When I went nearer, their long bovine tails
Flicked loosely, and deliberately they turned,
An undulation of dappled grey and brown,
And stood in profile with those curious planes
Of neck and sloping haunches. Just as when
Quite motionless they watched I never thought
Them moved by fear, a desire to be a tree,
So as they put more ground between us I
Saw evidence that these were animals with
Perhaps no wish for intercourse, or no
Capacity.
        Above the falling sun
Like visible winds the clouds are streaked and spun,

And cold and dark now bring the image of
Those creatures walking without pain or love.

c. 1944   ROY FULLER

The Mahratta Ghats

The valleys crack and burn, the exhausted plains
Sink their black teeth into the horny veins
Straggling the hills' red thighs, the bleating goats
– Dry bents and bitter thistles in their throats –
Thread the loose rocks by immemorial tracks.
Dark peasants drag the sun upon their backs.

High on the ghat the new turned soil is red,
The sun has ground it to the finest red,
It lies like gold within each horny hand.
Siva has spilt his seed upon this land.

Will she who burns and withers on the plain
Leave, ere too late, her scraggy herds of pain,
The cow-dung fire and the trembling beasts,
The little wicked gods, the grinning priests,
And climb, before a thousand years have fled,
High as the eagle to her mountain bed
Whose soil is fine as flour and blood-red?

But no! She cannot move. Each arid patch
Owns the lean folk who plough and scythe and thatch
Its grudging yield and scratch its stubborn stones.
The small gods suck the marrow from their bones.

Who is it climbs the summit of the road?
Only the beggar bumming his dark load.

Who was it cried to see the falling star?
Only the landless soldier lost in war.

And did a thousand years go by in vain?
And does another thousand start again?

c. 1945   ALUN LEWIS

By the Middle Sea

Above the agile giggling Arabs, the ageing palm
Fulfils her orbit. Wind and roots in their agreement
Grant her so much sphere. This way and that
She bends, formal yet graceful and even vivacious.

Like the attenuated wave that tosses the nervous yellow
    crabs
And hurries away. Then returns a little later
To reclaim its busy passengers.

Like the squat *flamboyant*, which reaches
Its scarlet flowers to passing lorries, and cheerfully
Spares them to blaze and bruise in the dirty street.

It is the sea and the trees amaze us, not
The eclectic bird, the migratory leviathan, or the
    wind-blown scrap of paper:
It is the arc of the swaying palm-tree that contains
A world, the thin white edge of a dying wave
That shakes with an ocean's energy. I remember
The terrible words of the admonitory master:
                                   'Free – for what?'

p. 1947   D. J. ENRIGHT

150

Beggar

Old as a coat on a chair; and his crushed hand,
as unexpressive as a bird's face, held
out like an offering, symbol of the blind,
he gropes our noise for charity. You could build
his long-deserted face up out of sand,
    or bear his weakness as a child.

Shuffling the seconds of a drugged watch, he
attends no answer to his rote; for soul's
and body's terrible humility,
stripped year by year a little barer, wills
nothing: he claims no selfhood in his cry:
    his body is an age that feels.

As if a mask, a tattered blanket, should
live for a little before falling, when
the body leaves it: so briefly in his dead
feathers of rags, and rags of body, and in
his crumpled mind, the awful and afraid
    stirs and pretends to be a man.

Earth's degradation and the voice of earth;
colour of earth and clothed in it; his eyes
white pebbles blind with deserts; the long growth
of landscape in his body: as if these
or these dead acres horribly gave birth:
    here will fall from him like disguise.

Only a sad and humble motion keeps
the little space he is, himself: to row
his mindless caves with ritual hand and lips,

and wonder dimly at his guilt: with no
memory of it now: it was perhaps
    too fearful, or too long ago.

p. 1945   TERENCE TILLER

Mokomeh Ghat

In the cool shade by the communal pump
The old men sat all day
Chewing betel or sleeping;
To them the cynical parody
The monkeys played among the mocking branches
Was not in the least disconcerting.

It was only in the early evening
As the women came in a long slim line
To draw water from the reluctant handle,
The tin-tin of bangles on their feet,
That the weariness of centuries became apparent.

p. 1945   J. C. MOLLISON

Greek Excavations

Over the long-shut house
Which earth, not keys kept under watch,
I prod with a stick and down comes rattling soil
Into the dug out room;
And pottery comes down,
Hard edges of drinking vessels, jars for oil,
Mere kitchen stuff, rubbish of red or brown,

Stubble of conquests
– And I suddenly discover this discovered town.

The wish of the many, their abused trust,
Blows down here in a little dust,
So much unpainted clay:
The minimum wish
For the permanence of the basic things of a life,
For children and friends and having enough to eat
And the great key of a skill;
The life the generals and the bankers cheat.

Peering for coin or confident bust
Or vase in bloom with the swiftness of horses,
My mind was never turned the way
Of the classic of the just and the unjust.
I was looking for things which have a date,
And less of the earth's weight,
When I broke this crust.

p. 1945   BERNARD SPENCER

Sea of Marmora

Beneath this sea forgotten voices dwell,
    in darkness murmur still their changeless words
of prayer or pleasure, clear in field and cell.

In stones incorporate the voices linger,
    stones from surrendered walls by Time subdued,
and beckoned far from light by the sea's finger:

153

man-shaped stone of monastic house and church,
 flint and crumbling earth of a planted field,
withdrawn from daylight and the sky's research,

are locked within the water's glass and frame.
 Where we now sail, melon and fig-tree grew
a thousand years before our voices came

to shake this evening's calm like eager birds
 gay in the light, the amber placid sea,
and add our English speech to distant words

that still live on beside the rusted blades,
 the sand-filled wine jars, tumbled bricks and stones
buried within the water's silent glades.

Now those monastic men and we are one
 this summer evening silent as a well,
while voices mingle, speak from sun to sun.

Like theirs, our words are taken by these shores,
 accepted by the grasses and the sea;
secured for ever by the steadfast doors

of the Earth's silence, they are stored at peace
 within the veins of stone, the clay's slow blood,
and safe with Time, from Time have their release.

p. 1947   ALEXANDER HENDERSON

African Village

Here history is dwarfed, the shape of Time
walks like a dark race through the tall, wild grass,
a child squats nakedly before a house
and draws the earth into its ancient eyes.
Thus would a tribal God reject the world,
turn from an empire with this secret smile
and raise a small hand to the mighty sun.
Out of the mud-shack water-proofed with tin
an old crone leans her leathern, empty breasts
once melon round and rich with mother's milk,
the teeming continent has drawn away;
when all has gone she knows she will remain.

Night comes upon them like an evil friend
to work his magic and to beat his drums
into the savage rhythm of their blood,
kindling a red fire and a leaping dance
where men are turned to shadows of the trees,
their limbs ecstatic in a lustful trance.
Night and the deep, receptive women of the tribe
lie and conceive the death of history,
which sprang from this first primitive embrace
and shall return into this fleshy womb.
But morning comes and brings the brassy sun
to burn its seed into the savage earth,
and hold communion with the ancient child
who stares at nothing with his inward eyes.

c. 1948   EMANUEL LITVINOFF

The Jungle

I

In mole-blue indolence the sun
Plays idly on the stagnant pool
In whose grey bed black swollen leaf
Holds Autumn rotting like an unfrocked priest.
The crocodile slides from the ochre sand
And drives the great translucent fish
Under the boughs across the running gravel.
Windfalls of brittle mast crunch as we come
To quench more than our thirst – our selves –
Beneath this bamboo bridge, this mantled pool
Where sleep exudes a sinister content
As though all strength of mind and limb must pass
And all fidelities and doubts dissolve,
The weighted word a bubble in each head,
The warm pacts of the flesh betrayed
By the nonchalance of a laugh,
The green indifference of this sleep.

II

Wandering and fortuitous the paths
We followed to this rendezvous today
Out of the mines and offices and dives,
The sidestreets of anxiety and want,
Huge cities known and distant as the stars,
Wheeling beyond our destiny and hope.
We did not notice how the accent changed
As shadows ride from precipice to plain
Closing the parks and cordoning the roads,
Clouding the humming cultures of the West –
The weekly bribe we paid the man in black,

The day shift sinking from the sun,
The blinding arc of rivets blown through steel,
The patient queues, headlines and slogans flung
Across a frightened continent, the town
Sullen and out of work, the little home
Semi-detached, suburban, transient
As fever or the anger of the old,
The best ones on some specious pretext gone.

But we who dream beside this jungle pool
Prefer the instinctive rightness of the poised
Pied kingfisher deep darting for a fish
To all the banal rectitude of states,
The dew-bright diamonds on a viper's back
To the slow poison of a meaning lost
And the vituperations of the just.

III

The banyan's branching clerestories close
The noon's harsh splendour to a head of light.
The black spot in the focus grows and grows:
The vagueness of the child, the lover's deep
And inarticulate bewilderment,
The willingness to please that made a wound,
The kneeling darkness and the hungry prayer;
Cargoes of anguish in the holds of joy,
The smooth deceitful stranger in the heart,
The tangled wrack of motives drifting down
An oceanic tide of Wrong.
And though the state has enemies we know
The greater enmity within ourselves.

Some things we cleaned like knives in earth,
Kept from the dew and rust of Time

Instinctive truths and elemental love,
Knowing the force that brings the teal and quail
From Turkestan across the Himalayan snows
To Kashmir and the South alone can guide
That winging wildness home again.

Oh you who want us for ourselves,
Whose love can start the snow-rush in the woods
And melt the glacier in the dark coulisse,
Forgive this strange inconstancy of soul,
The face distorted in a jungle pool
That drowns its image in a mort of leaves.

IV

Grey monkeys gibber, ignorant and wise.
We are the ghosts, and they the denizens;
We are like them anonymous, unknown,
Avoiding what is human, near,
Skirting the villages, the paddy fields
Where boys sit timelessly to scare the crows
On bamboo platforms raised above their lives.

A trackless wilderness divides
Joy from its cause, the motive from the act:
The killing arm uncurls, strokes the soft moss;
The distant world is an obituary,
We do not hear the tappings of its dread.
The act sustains; there is no consequence.
Only aloneness, swinging slowly
Down the cold orbit of an older world
Than any they predicted in the schools,
Stirs the cold forest with a starry wind,
And sudden as the flashing of a sword
The dream exalts the bowed and golden head

And time is swept with a great turbulence,
The old temptation to remould the world.

The bamboos creak like an uneasy house;
The night is shrill with crickets, cold with space.
And if the mute pads on the sand should lift
Annihilating paws and strike us down
Then would some unimportant death resound
With the imprisoned music of the soul?
And we become the world we could not change?

Or does the will's long struggle end
With the last kindness of a foe or friend?

c. 1945   ALUN LEWIS

Wild Olive

Once the olive grew out of the tower,
Once the breeze on the evening sea
Darkened the solitary lover.

Time is a faceless statue of stone,
The unasked guest at the feast,
The tree that outlives our love

Like death we cannot forget,
Or peace for a passing moment
Between the thought and the wind.

c. 1947   WREY GARDINER

Phileremo

A philosopher in search of human values
Might have seen something in the coarse
Black boots the guide wore when he led us:
Boots with cracked eyes and introspective
Laces, rich in historical error as this
Old wall we picked the moss from, reading
Into it invasions by the Dorians or Medes.

But the bearded arboreal historian
Saw nothing of it all, was nothing then.
His education had derailed the man
Until he moved, a literary reminiscence,
Through quotations only, fine as hair.

The stones spoke to him. Reflected there
In a cistern I heard you thinking: Europe
Also, the whole of our egopetal culture
Is done for and must vanish soon.

And still we have not undergone the poet's truth.

Could we comfort us in more than this
Blue sea and air cohering blandly
Across that haze of flats,
The smoking middens of our history –
Aware perhaps only of the two children
Asleep in the car beside a bear in cotton gloves?

c. 1948   LAWRENCE DURRELL

On a Carved Axle-piece from a Sicilian Cart

The village craftsman stirred his bravest yellow
and (all the carpentry and carving done)
put the last touches to his newest cart,
until no playing-card had brighter panels;
with crested knights in armour, king and crown
Crusaders slaughtering infidels, and crimson
where the blood laves:
and took his paintpot to that part
around the axle where a Southern memory
harking back out of Christendom, imagined
a chariot of glory
and Aphrodite riding wooden waves.

So some tanned peasant paid his money down
and till the years
put a full-stop to him or his purchase, jaunted
half around Sicily with wood for the fire,
long muscat grapes
or tangerines for the market in the town.
Thus answering, as his fathers' fathers had,
those metaphysical gaps and fears
which drain the blood of the age or drive it mad;
Who is God? Where do I come from? Are we dying?

– With a salty way of speech; with tasselled harness
with a cart to match the sea and all the flowers;
with Roger the Christian and Palermo towers;
and in between the dusty wheels
the Queen of Love in a yellow gown,
featured like a peasant child,

her three red horses rearing from the foam
and their carved manes blown wild.

p. 1947   BERNARD SPENCER

Greek Archipelagoes

Crete
Smoulders on sea, half-way to Africa,
Solitary phoenix of the Aegean brood.
Songs, shouts echo in a lunar wilderness
Where blood flowers on the knuckles of the mountains.
High in the ilex woods the black riflemen stalk
Waking the din of bells; their jangling shots
Uncoil interminable echoes. Here the hands of friends
Grasp yours for ever.

Stone warrior up to the waist in sea
Blue as an eye and circled by the blood
Of minotaur and janissary and german!
The wild goat leaps from biceps to armoured shoulder,
And fossilized whiskers are a perch for eagles.
The iron eye of Ida
Looks towards Africa, the empty road
Where no ship travels and the Libyan moon
Only moves: the liquid desert
That hides with the hazard of an excavation
Forests of sponges, ringed by the tunnelling plunge
Of men from Kalymnos, who, taut as miners,
Work underwater.

*

Count Spiridion and the noble Dionysios,
Gonfaloniers of the Doge, walk down a silver stair
Falter a moment by the looking-glass

To lisp a rumour of the Mocenigo.
They puff their lace out, poising fastidious fingers
On hilts of swords they never draw. The flicker
Of paste buckles underneath a scutcheon
Marks their way through barley-sugar columns
Into the grape-green evening. There
Lanterns in olive trees cast spokes of shade
On lawns that slope to the sea. The lanterned boats
Scatter the sound of mandolines on pearl-smooth water.

These are Corfu and Zante. Their balustrades,
Magnolias and aloe-flowers are pale as snow
Under a benevolent zodiac.
These islands float like aloe petals
On the Ionian, as though a south wind might
Blow them away, baring the western sea
Of the italianate septinsular galaxy.
All but that dismal and preposterous mountain
Those villages peopled by statues of shipowners,
Where, on the limestone crags, gesticulate
The lunatics of Cephalonia.

*

Nothing seems older than the Cyclades
Worn by the world's earliest winds, thumbed smooth by
    legend,
They are the seamarks of history,
Offering columns like an instrument
To the wind's mouth; and these oleanders once gave shade
To kings and philosophers that have left
Not even, or nothing but, a name.
Bargains were struck by merchants on the quays
While the first heroes snored in the stifling marble
Awaiting the sculptor's chisel, the tap of a bird's beak
To hatch them.

                    They were stepping-stones to Troy
Trireme-harbours, milestones to Odysseys
A night's sleep for argonauts.
Their thoroughfares are stale with a million keels
Weaving and looping their course like wool-winders
Round the porous, the salty fingertips
Of a gigantic and drowned skeleton, jutting here
A bleached knee or a rib; or charred eye-socket
Like Santorin.
Santorin,
Curling and smoky and satanic
Fires a spiral ladder in the air
And balances a town among the birds.

                         *

Ἐν ἀρχῇ ἦν ὁ Λόγος
From the north
The autumn wind carries the storks over Patmos
From Kiev and Bukovina, Rila and the Euxine,
Mystra and Athos and the hanging Meteora,
Stretching their necks for Sinai. The slow armada
Tangles the passage of the Word of God:
A load of plumed and shifting fruit
Bends the branches of the only tree.

The Word of God split the rocks here
And built this battlemented monastery
On rocks that are Magians cast down and turned to
    stone,
To hide the Word, the leisure of the monks
From scimitars of the corsairs, a stone casket
For treasure of Constantinople and the Russias,
Mitres and flasks and chrysobuls and scrolls,
Gifts of half-legendary voivodes, and the crosiers
Of bishops who became saints.

(Foreheads of parchment seen in silver coffins,
Palimpsests where the flourishes of mortality are faded
Under the calligraphy of beatitude.)

The wind in the soaking darkness winds
Through rocks and roofs, lifting the unwilling wing
Of huddling storks.
Thunder explodes, and the shuddering apocalypse
Of lightning bares the shapes of cupolas
The mountain-side and rain-logged wings
And tethered caïques that rear like frightened horses.

*

On an Aegean rock compound of salt
And oil and lizards, the bent mastick-tree
Under the sun's tread spills a lingering tear.
The press destroys the olive. A gold tooth
Sparkles in the dark under a tired forehead
Striped like a tiger with the wipe of fingers
Where the oil clings. Fingers that are fossils
Roll a cigarette; juice streams from ankles
Into the trodden vine-stalks among the jars
And the must grumbles and hits, sending fumes as
    startling
Into the vaults, as the sudden movement of the heart's
Split-second scaffolding of a poem
Assembling in the skull's archways.

                              The spite of the sun
Splinters the disc of shade the olive casts,
Crumples the fetishes of the carob-tree
That hang in haze and dazzle the track of the eye
Under the ilex to the sea,
The sea that gasps for sunset.

These stones and thorns, that stone without a shadow,
Are ambiguous emblems, they are
Half-decipherable runes, notes in a tune
That can't be memorized. (The unrancorous
Moon will rise over an unsolved problem.)

The donkey waiting under a load of jars
Under the prickly-pear and the white walls
Of this necropolis brays without an echo
To stir the rare blue waterfalls of shade.
There is nothing here, nothing at all.
Only, perhaps, a question or a mood
A reference or a suggestion,
Rocks and the sun, and pastures for dolphins
Scattered with other islands, old and bare
As jutting bones, recent as thunderbolts.

Unfathomable wells
Tunnel the heart of the pumice. Like a hand
The fig leaf lays a shadow on the dust.

These islands are the end of a hundred worlds.

p. 1949   PATRICK LEIGH FERMOR

Italy

The veins of water
in this dark peninsula
are sentimental with lanterns
and the ends of sentences.
The sun's hot needles
hold lizards and butterflies
on the foreheads of statues

and under the misery
of the heart, where the orange
lips of girls press the wax
image there of a poem
and leave no traces
of the corrupted happiness.
Stars crumble in water. The mouth
of the river holds the musical
starlight. The rooms beyond
are the rooms of the dead
where the captured horror
of cactus and sand
is made into serenity
of thorn and dryness in the end
become a fountain and a cup
and the whole of heaven
inclined into the throat.
The foliate cities
tread on fans of mimosa
and thrust their organs
through the upward playing
of water and sunlight. Over
their love and their exhausted sleeping
the far-off orchestra
in the mind hints of liberty.
O correction of music
calm our lives with your swallows
weaving over our eyes
the same ripple of evening,
that securely remembers
the more northern cities
and the roofs where birds
sang in the white mornings.
O poet in rags
O poet clutching your roses

insensible under the wound
of your belief in Man
write on our faces
the cerise entanglement
of a word for evening
and a song for daybreak.

p. 1945   ERNEST FROST

On a Return from Egypt

To stand here in the wings of Europe
disheartened, I have come away
from the sick land where in the sun lay
the gentle sloe-eyed murderers
of themselves, exquisites under a curse;
here to exercise my depleted fury.

For the heart is a coal, growing colder
when jewelled cerulean seas change
into grey rocks, grey water-fringe,
sea and sky altering like a cloth
till colour and sheen are gone both:
cold is an opiate of the soldier.

And all my endeavours are unlucky explorers
come back, abandoning the expedition;
the specimens, the lilies of ambition
still spring in their climate, still unpicked:
but time, time is all I lacked
to find them, as the great collectors before me.

The next month, then, is a window
and with a crash I'll split the glass.
Behind it stands one I must kiss,
person of love or death
a person or a wraith,
I fear what I shall find.

Egypt–England, 1943–4   KEITH DOUGLAS
c. 1951

De Amicitia

Odysseus, at the end of life, in your orchards,
Stroking the olive-flowers and the young corn
With thin dry fingers – only in your eyes
The fire that once was the whole man – Odysseus,
Tell me, from all your travels
What do you most remember?

'Not Troy, not any thought of Troy.
Not Polypheme. Not Kalypso. Nor does the sea
Feature except as a well-honoured friend
Smiling a greeting but no invitation.

'More than all else I think of the Phaeacians,
Leisure and music in their halls,
The laughter of Alkinous and his tales,
The freedom and the peace of an old friendship,
    And Nausikaa,
                gay as hibiscus-bloom,
Fresher than dawn, shining unconscious foil
To my other world, to all the dross of manhood.'

24 April 1942   FRANK THOMPSON
c. 1947

169

'OPENING A WAY THROUGH TIME...'

Seance

The automatic fingers write. Tonight
We huddle round the table. Hands and features
Are green beneath the flicker of the light.
The pencil shakes, and bites into the future.

Then from the mouth, as from a rumbling cavern,
Reverberate the syllables of doom.
The body jerks away. In dense and driven
Rigor of ecstasy the fingers drum.

Anguish of drowning flesh! To see the blue
And swollen lips! The eye-balls burst, the skin
Sweats salt.   'Speak, speak to those who question you!'
The lamp-light thickens, and the voice begins:

'I see blood drying on a fissured rock
While all about the dark birds wheel and hover,
Image of death, image of all the black
Terrors of death that shall beset the lover.

'I see you in an empty room, while far
Away in unimagined valleys move
The bright and transitory shapes of war.
I see the endlessness and ache of love.

'I see the petrifaction of your lust,
Hands tearing, tearing ceaselessly at stone.
It is a stony image that you kiss.
You are alone, you always are alone.

'. . . You always are alone.' The murmur ceases,
The body tumbles sideways in the chair.

Beneath the light the green, distorted faces
Recoil in attitudes of mute despair.

Whose is the voice that fills the shadowed room?
Who drowns beneath the revelatory wind?
Mine are the swollen lips that speak of doom,
And mine the stiff and automatic hand.

p.1948   FRANCIS KING

Maria Aegyptiaca

Thrust back by hands of air from the sanctuary door,
Mary of Egypt, that hot whore,
Fell on the threshold-stone. Priest, candles, acolyte
Shivered in flame upon her failing sight –
She swooned, and lay there like one dead. And then she
    fled
In the black Thebaid. For forty years
She hid among the rocks splintered with heat;
The greedy desert to its own pitiless drought
Sucked all her body's beauty – which had spread
A wildfire death in kisses through brown limbs
Of sailormen at Alexandria,
Or Syrian fig-merchants with small dull eyes.
                              All night she would display
Her naked skin and bones to the harsh red moon
To be her only lover; through the day,
(While she was kneeling on the white hot sand)
Hairy and ithyphallic,
The dancing satyrs would distract her prayer;
The memory of her lust
Split open the rock-tombs, and buried kings
Whose brown dead flesh was like dried dates, with eyes

174

Of emerald glittering in a gilded mask,
Tripped forth, their grave-bands looped fantastically,
And made their court to her with antic bows.

.   .   .   .   .

And when at last she died,
With burning tender eyes, hair like dark flame,
The golden lion came;
And with his terrible claws scooped out a tomb,
Gently, in the loose soil,
And gave that dry burnt corpse to the earth's womb.

c. 1950   JOHN HEATH-STUBBS

The Brass Horse

Never presume that in this marble stable
Furnished with imitation stalactites,
Withheld from any manger and unable
To stamp impatient hooves or show the whites
Of eyes whose lids are fixed, on sulky nights
He asks himself no questions, has no doubt
What he a brazen engine is about.

Diving on some dry region when his rider
Twiddled the key in his untwitching ear,
Forced through his Himalayan paces, glider
Over the Gobi and the flat Pamir,
Trained by telepathy to disappear
And grow from nothing, he was well aware
Of exploitation and unloving care.

Do you suppose he had no means of knowing
The talking falcon and physician sword
That splinters all chainmail, the mirror showing

What slaughter is in store what golden hoard?
Nor as he automatically pawed
And snorted fire in the loud palace yard
Resented the wide-gaping mob's regard?

We cannot guess what thoughts of combination
With the decaying cayman on the wall
Or the snow leopard blinded by elation
Trouble him in his brahmin-carven stall,
For what Arabian mares and ribboned manes
He writhes his motionless metallic reins.

1942   DRUMMOND ALLISON
c. 1944

Troll Kings

O wake them not, the big-boned kings,
The sleepers and the sworded kings; the lonely
Inhuman kings who sit with drawn-up knees
Waiting with twisted eyes the time of terror.
O wake them not, the troll kings, the forgotten.

Seraphion the sleeper turns a tired
Metallic eyeball through the lacunae
Of the black tomb; and Arthur mumbles
The names of white-haired women, Guenever
Remembers, and her exhumation, bursting
Like a deep-buried mine on Avalon's touchy climate;
Lancelot too, the double lover, sees him
Riding the roads but rusty now his manners
And gaunt the horse, and white the horse he rides;
And the neurotic banners, and the guessed-at
Grail that was white and gracious as his hope.

Ragnar sleeps too, the great-sworded
King of the trolls, his language no more spoken
Now in the woods, except by winking squirrel
And furtive jay; lies battened
Under black rocks unknown to mole or miner.
Ragnar the ironmaster, O remember
Ragnar regretting the plump peasant girls
Who knew his kingdom and forgot the light.
So sleep the old troll kings, with Barbarossa
Who died on the sharp ice; with Attila
The Tartar buried in a northern forest;
With Alexander, the cold fugitive
From fame and politics; with all outmoded heroes.

O do not speak to them lest they rise up
One cold night under the moon to fight for us.
They wait a backward day: how should they know
Such folly as we suffer, such perplexity
Of soul, such deadly love, such wonder?
Then let them sleep, the poor things, this cold night.

November 1941   SIDNEY KEYES
c. 1945

Belshazzar

That day in the city there were banners slung
Across the streets, from balconies and chimneys,
Swinging in the wind like smoke, and telegraph poles
Were hung with geraniums; military bands
Marched down the thoroughfares and bugles rang
Against the plate-glass frontages. And in that night

177

There were fireworks in the public parks at twilight,
Laburnums of flame that flowered and fell through the
   air,
And high on the hill the palace windows blazed
Like the shell of a house on fire. And in that night
The uniforms moved along the lobbies, gold and scarlet,
Gold and blue, and shoulders were sugared with jewels
Under the hanging icicles of chandeliers.
They poured the yellow wine in the grey silver,
The red in the yellow gold, and plates were piled
With quails and nightingales and passion fruit,
And the air was a fume of music. And in that night
The King sat above his court, speaking to none,
Small and grotesque there in a high-backed chair,
His hands gripping the carved griffins, his eyes
Like halves of hard-boiled eggs. He stared at the wall,
At the bare plaster above the footmen's heads.
The music and laughter ceased, the people were silent,
They put down their forks and raised no cup to the mouth,
But turned and stared at the wall where the King was
   staring.
And there was nothing on the wall at all.

c. 1944   NORMAN NICHOLSON

The Wreck

(from a story by Hemingway)

He lived alone upon an island where
trees could not live, alone with sea and gulls
that cried all day and broke like snap of wire
into the sky; they saw him by their pools
kick the dead crabs that lay between tide-lulls.

But one day came the wind out of the west
and drove the spiteful spray from rock to cloud,
and when the winter storm was at its worst
a liner bound for home with all its load
leaped up against the rock like a grey toad
and sank upon the sand, and lay as still
as a black stone lies down a disused shaft
or stalagmite, or a dead animal.
The man turned over in his sleep and laughed
touching the empty space upon his left.

Next morning when the sea went slowly by
he took his boat and rowed to where the birds
beat at each other in a patch of grey
above the wreck, quarrelling landwards
with quick peck and uncanny scream of words.

They scattered as he drew where they had been
and there he saw, shadowed from bow to stern,
dark from the rock, distinct and clear as bone,
the quiet ship leaning against the stone,
leaving the glassy water without stain.

Catching his breath, he dived to where she lay
and tried to break a port-hole in her side,
could not, but as he had to break away,
saw a woman's white face and hair inside
bright as the king of Argos' golden bride.

Hair like the golden willow dipping low
in river water from a field of green,
or like gold tracery of long ago –
Byzantine, Babylonian found again,
beauty that strikes with unexpected pain.

He swam for air, but soon he dived to see
if she had gone, again he struck the glass,
it would not break; he struck insistently,
forgetting she was dead; he could not guess
how soon her face would fade into a mask.

Day after day he saw her beauty fade,
break into pieces, turn and slowly rot:
the eyes went soon, only the gold hair stayed
a little longer, like a broken net
half-covering the black shape that it set.

Then this too went, but he came back each day
to shoot the gulls above the breaking wreck,
and scream delighted if he saw one die;
each evening he thought her beauty back
but when he dreamed, the face and hair turned black.

c. 1943   JOHN BAYLISS

The Healing of the Leper

O, have you seen the leper healed,
And fixed your eyes upon his look?
There is the book of God revealed,
And God has made no other book.

The withered hand which time interred
Grasps in a moment the unseen.
The word we had not heard, is heard.
What we are then, we had not been.

Plotinus, preaching on heaven's floor,
Could not give praise like that loud cry

Bursting the bondage of death's door;
For we die once; indeed we die.

What Sandro Botticelli found
Rose from the river where we bathe:
Music the air, the stream, the ground;
Music the dove, the rock, the faith.

And all that music whirled upon
The eyes' deep-sighted, burning rays,
Where all the prayers of labours done
Are resurrected into praise.

But look: his face is like a mask
Surrounded by the beat of wings.
Because he knows that ancient task
His true transfiguration springs.

All fires the prophets' words contained
Fly to those eyes, transfixed above.
Their awful precept has remained:
'Be nothing, first; and then, be love.'

c. 1948   VERNON WATKINS

Christ Walking on the Water

Slowly, O so slowly, longing rose up
In the forenoon of his face, till only
A ringlet of fog lingered round his loins;
And fast he went down beaches all weeping
With weed, and waded out. Twelve tall waves
Sequent and equated, hollowed and followed.
O what a cock-eyed sea he walked on,

What poke-ends of foam, what elbowings
And lugubrious looks, what ebullient
And contumacious musics. Always there were
Hills and holes, pills and poles, a wavy wall
And bucking ribbon caterpillaring past
With glossy ease. And often, as he walked,
The slow curtains of swell swung open and showed,
Miles and smiles away, the bottle-boat
Flung on one wavering frond of froth that fell
Knee-deep and heaved thigh-high. In his forward face
No cave of afterthought opened; to his ear
No bottom clamour climbed up; nothing blinked.
For he was the horizon, he the hub,
Both bone and flesh, finger and ring of all
This clangorous sea. Docile, at his toe's touch,
Each tottering dot stood roundaboutly calm
And jammed the following others fast as stone.
The ironical wave smoothed itself out
To meet him, and the mocking hollow
Hooped its back for his feet. A spine of light
Sniggered on the knobbly water, ahead.
But he like a lover, caught up,
Pushed past all wrigglings and remonstrances
And entered the rolling belly of the boat
That shuddered and lay still. And he lay there
Emptied of his errand, oozing still. Slowly
The misted mirror of his eyes grew clear
And cold, the bell of blood tolled lower,
And bright before his sight the ocean bared
And rolled its horrible bold eye-balls endlessly
In round rebuke. Looking over the edge
He shivered. Was this the way he had come?
Was that the one who came? The backward bowl
And all the bubble-pit that he had walked on
Burst like a plate into purposelessness.

All, all was gone, the fervour and the froth
Of confidence, and flat as water was
The sad and glassy round. Somewhere, then,
A tiny flute sounded, O so lonely.
A ring of birds rose up and wound away
Into nothingness. Beyond himself he saw
The settled steeples, and breathing beaches
Running with people. But he,
He was custodian to nothing now,
And boneless as an empty sleeve hung down.
Down from crowned noon to cambered evening
He fell, fell, from white to amber, till night
Slid over him like an eyelid. And he,
His knees drawn up, his head dropped deep,
Curled like a question-mark, asleep.

p. 1943   W. R. RODGERS

Seven Dreams

Breaking through the first door, he found
a still lake, luminous by the sallow moon,
burnished with green fire along its banks,
and heard the dry wind beating the bulrush stems,
and there were dead birds in this dream.

But in the next he was a great emperor,
a winged moth over white water,
dizzy with love of the moon's reflection,
and entered to restore the green
emerald under the moonstone lying,
pierced the dark layer but could not breathe –
his lovely wings folding and fading. . . .

And later he slept one night lapped in water,
Moses in darkness, as quiet as sleeping moorhen
soft in the shadow by the still shore.

And again he moved with four horsemen
over the stone bridge, the stream leading
into the lake, and left them,
going to gather them water,
seeing a grey swan like a cloud gliding,
and by now he had reached the fifth door.

Which opened on to a brown arcade of fruits
– apricot and mulberry, nectarine, peach,
grape and gold orange by the singing tree,
and there peacocks walked by the fountains
pecking the bright fruit disdainfully,
and he saw the green lake against tall mountains.

But the sixth door led into a dark tower,
a spider had obscured the names on the wall
and water drawn moss over them,
and a black knight stood in the hall,
and against the stairs the echoes rang
as if they were following him,
and the top of the tower shook like a mast,
and the lake was covered by a black mist.

And the last door was without a key
but it lay open to the touch of fingers,
showing the choir of a church,
but he found no singers:
and here lay the fruit like wax
offerings to the red moon,
and he saw the four horsemen
engraved on a grey tomb;
and, glowing in stained glass,

the several peacocks stood
admiring themselves in swan's blood,
and he saw the moth dying
in the fading tree, and the black knight beneath
awaiting its last breath;
then a black bat flying disturbed him
and he thought with dismay of the eighth dream
seeing the lake through the small doorway. . . .

c. 1943   JOHN BAYLISS

Lazarus

This knock means death. I heard it once before
As I was struggling to remember one,
Just one thing, crying in my fever for
Help, help. Then the door opened, yet no Son

Came in to whisper what I had to know.
Only my sisters wetted me with tears,
But tears are barren symbols. Love is slow,
And when she comes she neither speaks nor hears:

She only kisses and revives the dead
Perhaps in vain. Because what is the use
Of miracles unheard-of, since instead
Of trying to remember the great News

Revealed to me alone by Death and Love,
I struggled to forget them and become
Like everybody else? I longed to move
As if I never had been overcome

By mysteries which made my sisters shiver
As they prepared the supper for our Friend.

He came and we received Him as the Giver,
But did not ask Him when our joy would end.

And now I hear the knock I heard before,
And strive to make up for the holy time,
But I cannot remember, and the door
Creaks letting in my unambiguous crime.

c. 1947   DEMETRIOS CAPETANAKIS

Lust

Lovely Actaeon to the lake
Broke through the pathless wood,
In sexual pride to spy upon
Diana's maidenhood.

He forced the last tree-limbs apart –
Stood slobbering like an oaf,
Fumbled and sweated on the bank
Then turned and bolted off.

His senses numb he hardly knew
The fresh four-legged tread,
Nor stag upon the body grown
Nor antlers on the head;

But hears the baying of his hounds
And quivering turns to fly:
What pride bid limbs to stand at last,
Welcomed that swelling cry?

c. 1946   PATRIC DICKINSON

Relics

In that stone head, obscenity
Has been preserved a thousand years;
A bible-leaf of families
Have shuddered at the pointed ears.

The sword that hangs upon the wall
Is notched the length of its long blade,
And children at the village school
Dream of the trusses it has mowed.

Close against the lichened tower
Still lives a witch. Around her head
She wears a shawl, and white as flour
Her lips count every step she treads.

But when the dusk-born lovers stand
The figure sobs, 'Oh where's my soul?',
The sword sighs for the long-dead hand,
The old hag huddles from the owl.

c. 1945   HENRY TREECE

Wade

After the league of ogres hurtling logs
Against him as he climbed the cloven hills,
The serpent served with virgins in hot halls,
The barge bewitched and rowed by idiot dogs

He knelt unweeping at his father's tomb
Working out ways to cheat his ancestors;

He sliced his acres up, tore down the towers
And shared their thankless tasks with guard and groom:

Expunged from song the hero of The Churls,
Mentioned by Malory when absent-minded,
And no lies left about his grief amended
Who died refused by henwives and goosegirls.

1942   DRUMMOND ALLISON
c. 1944

Abel

My brother Cain, the wounded, liked to sit
Brushing my shoulder, by the staring water
Of life, or death, in cinemas half-lit
By scenes of peace that always turned to slaughter.

He liked to talk to me. His eager voice
Whispered the puzzle of his bleeding thirst,
Or prayed me not to make my final choice,
Unless we had a chat about it first.

And then he chose the final pain for me.
I do not blame his nature: he's my brother;
Nor what you call the times: our love was free,
Would be the same at any time; but rather

The ageless ambiguity of things
Which makes our life mean death, our love be hate.
My blood that streams across the bedroom sings:
'I am my brother opening the gate!'

p. 1943   DEMETRIOS CAPETANAKIS

188

Good Friday

Today the willowed river grieves,
The mountains are in funeral black,
The dove is hushed among the leaves,
The worm has halted in his track,
And glassy-eyed a frosted hare
Is lying strangled in a snare.

Red in the brackened wood below,
The old fox hears his judgment horn,
He sees the bobbing huntsmen go
Across the meadows raped of corn,
And gasping in the trampled reeds
A wounded salmon slowly bleeds.

c. 1948   LEONARD CLARK

Sour Land

At Stanton Harcourt in Oxfordshire there is an
ancient tower in which Pope completed the fifth
book of his *Iliad*, when illness and disillusionment
were beginning to oppress him.

I

The houses are white stone in this country,
Windowless and blind as leprosy;
No peace for the wanderer waiting only death.
Plovers crouch in the rain between the furrows
Or wheel club-winged and tumble across the wind;
A land so dead ghosts lodge not
Along its borders to torment the mind.
No ghosts, but another terror; every naked road

189

Of this sour land harbours a running demon
Who jogs along the fallow all night long
Black under moonlit cloud though shadowless;
Even by day the acrid-tasting air
Reveals his presence to the introspective.
The ponds are cloudy, filled with eyeshot corpses
Of servant girls who drowned themselves for spite.
This landscape of bulbous elm and stubble
Sharpens the mind into revolt at last.

II

So to his perch appropriate with owls
The old lame poet would repair,
When sorrow like a tapeworm in his bowels
Drove him to Troy and other men's despair.

His lame leg twisted on the spiral stair,
He cursed the harsher canker in his heart;
Then in the turret he would scrawl and glare
And long to pull his enemies apart.

When night came knocking at the panes
And bats' thin screeching pierced his head,
He thought of copulation in the lanes
And bit his nails and praised the glorious dead.

At dawn the lapwings cried and he awoke
From dreams of Paris drowned in Helen's hair;
He drew his pride about him like a cloak
To face again the agony of the stair.

III

O friend, if you should venture to that country,
Pass guardedly, be unseduced
By its too subtle promises of peace;

Its quiet is of a kind you should not seek.
Look not about you overmuch
Nor listen by the churchyard wall
Lest you should hear the words as soft as nightfall
Of death in promises kind but lecherous indeed.
Heed not the spirit of the twisted ash
Who counsels how to tie the noose;
Neither the spirit calling under the bridge
Where the long eel-grass twists to strangulation.
The sullen girl who smiles and shows her teeth
Is rather more than the common type of slut:
The old man ploughing against the wind
Turns over more than soil; or in the pasture
Two men are digging not a trench –
A grave for all you know and all you hope.
Remember the weasel questing down the hedge,
The dead crow hanging from the oak.
This is a very ancient land indeed;
Aiaia formerly or Cythera
Or Celidon the hollow forest called;
This is the country Ulysses and Hermod
Entered afraid; by ageing poets sought
Where lives no love nor any kind of flower
Only the running demon, thought.

November 1940   SIDNEY KEYES
c. 1945

The Patient

    Unvisited, unseen,
A stone into the ochre distance rolled,
The house lay burning in a sand-dune's fold,
    And nothing passed between –

191

Nothing between dark eyes and ocean's darker green.
Like waves, blank and unreckoned,
The minutes thudded downward on his brain,
Each with its raw, rasped undertow of pain,
Till, strangely, for a second
It seemed as if a distant figure stood and beckoned.

Into remembrance thrust
Like some archaic torso in the sand
Naked and desolate it seemed to stand.
He started. What sudden gust
Had blown this hope from hopelessness, this life from
dust?

Someone he once had known!
Yet as his parched lips started calling, calling,
He saw the figure drifting, dimming, falling.
His cry thinned to a moan.
He felt the house crash back on him, a burning stone.

But though all trace had gone,
His eyes still held their fixed, unwinking stare
Against the sand-dune's and the ocean's glare.
Above, the sun still shone
And still the raw, rasped minutes thudded on and on.

p. 1948   FRANCIS KING

Envoi

Take of me what is not my own,
my love, my beauty, and my poem,
the pain is mine, and mine alone.

See how against the weight in the bone
the hawk hangs perfect in mid-air –
the blood pays dear to raise it there,
the moment, not the bird, divine.

And see the peaceful trees extend
their myriad leaves in leisured dance –
they bear the weight of sky and cloud
upon the fountain of the veins.

In rose with petals light as air
I bind for you the tides and fire –
the death that lives within the flower
oh gladly, love, for you I bear.

p. 1942   KATHLEEN RAINE

Bird

O bird that was my vision,
my love, my dream that flew
over the famine-folded rocks,
the sky's reflected snow.

O bird that found and fashioned me,
that brought me from the land
safe in her singing cage of bone,
the webbed wings of her hand.

She took me to the topmost air,
curled in the atom of her eye,
and there I saw an island rise
out of the empty sea.

193

And falling there she set me down
naked on soil that knew no plough,
and loveless, speechless, I beheld
the world's beginning grow.

And there I slew her for my bread
and in her feathers dressed;
and there I raised a paradise
from the seed in her dead breast.

p. 1946   LAURIE LEE

A Winter's Tale

It is a winter's tale
That the snow blind twilight ferries over the lakes
And floating fields from the farm in the cup of the vales,
Gliding windless through the hand folded flakes,
The pale breath of cattle at the stealthy sail,

And the stars falling cold,
And the smell of hay in the snow, and the far owl
Warning among the folds, and the frozen hold
Flocked with the sheep white smoke of the farm house
    cowl
In the river wended vales where the tale was told.

Once when the world turned old
On a star of faith pure as the drifting bread,
As the food and flames of the snow, a man unrolled
The scrolls of fire that burned in his heart and head,
Torn and alone in a farm house in a fold

Of fields. And burning then
In his firelit island ringed by the winged snow
And the dung hills white as wool and the hen
Roosts sleeping chill till the flame of the cock crow
Combs through the mantled yards and the morning men

Stumble out with their spades,
The cattle stirring, the mousing cat stepping shy,
The puffed birds hopping and hunting, the milkmaids
Gentle in their clogs over the fallen sky,
And all the woken farm at its white trades,

He knelt, he wept, he prayed,
By the spit and the black pot in the log bright light
And the cup and the cut bread in the dancing shade,
In the muffled house, in the quick of night,
At the point of love, forsaken and afraid.

He knelt on the cold stones,
He wept from the crest of grief, he prayed to the veiled
    sky
May his hunger go howling on bare white bones
Past the statues of the stables and the sky roofed sties
And the duck pond glass and the blinding byres alone

Into the home of prayers
And fires where he should prowl down the cloud
Of his snow blind love and rush in the white lairs.
His naked need struck him howling and bowed
Though no sound flowed down the hand folded air

But only the wind strung
Hunger of birds in the fields of the bread of water, tossed
In high corn and the harvest melting on their tongues.
And his nameless need bound him burning and lost
When cold as snow he should run the wended vales among

The rivers mouthed in night,
And drown in the drifts of his need, and lie curled
    caught
In the always desiring centre of the white
Inhuman cradle and the bride bed forever sought
By the believer lost and the hurled outcast of light.

Deliver him, he cried,
By losing him all in love, and cast his need
Alone and naked in the engulfing bride,
Never to flourish in the fields of the white seed
Or flower under the time dying flesh astride.

Listen. The minstrels sing
In the departed villages. The nightingale,
Dust in the buried wood, flies on the grains of her wings
And spells on the winds of the dead his winter's tale.
The voice of the dust of water from the withered spring

Is telling. The wizened
Stream with bells and baying water bounds. The dew
    rings
On the gristed leaves and the long gone glistening
Parish of snow. The carved mouths in the rock are wind
    swept strings.
Time sings through the intricately dead snow drop. Listen.

It was a hand or sound
In the long ago land that glided the dark door wide
And there outside on the bread of the ground
A she bird rose and rayed like a burning bride.
A she bird dawned, and her breast with snow and
    scarlet downed.

Look. And the dancers move
On the departed, snow bushed green, wanton in moon
    light

As a dust of pigeons. Exulting, the rave hooved
Horses, centaur dead, turn and tread the drenched white
Paddocks in the farms of birds. The dead oak walks for
  love.

       The carved limbs in the rock
Leap, as to trumpets. Calligraphy of the old
Leaves is dancing. Lines of age on the stones weave in
  a flock.
And the harp shaped voice of the water's dust plucks in
  a fold
Of fields. For love, the long ago she bird rises. Look.

       And the wild wings were raised
Above her folded head, and the soft feathered voice
Was flying through the house as though the she bird
  praised
And all the elements of the slow fall rejoiced
That a man knelt alone in the cup of the vales,

       In the mantle and calm,
By the spit and the black pot in the log bright light.
And the sky of birds in the plumed voice charmed
Him up and he ran like a wind after the kindling flight
Past the blind barns and byres of the windless farm.

       In the poles of the year
When black birds died like priests in the cloaked hedge
  row
And over the cloth of counties the far hills rode near,
Under the one leaved trees ran a scarecrow of snow
And fast through the drifts of the thickets antlered like
  deer,

       Rags and prayers down the knee-
Deep hillocks and loud on the numbed lakes,

All night lost and long wading in the wake of the she-
Bird through the times and lands and tribes of the slow
    flakes.
Listen and look where she sails the goose plucked sea,

       The sky, the bird, the bride,
The cloud, the need, the planted stars, the joy beyond
The fields of seed and the time dying flesh astride,
The heavens, the heaven, the grave, the burning font.
In the far ago land the door of his death glided wide,

       And the bird descended.
On a bread white hill over the cupped farm
And the lakes and floating fields and the river wended
Vales where he prayed to come to the last harm
And the home of prayers and fires, the tale ended.

       The dancing perishes
On the white, no longer growing green, and, minstrel
    dead,
The singing breaks in the snow shoed villages of wishes
That once cut the figures of birds on the deep bread
And over the glazed lakes skated the shapes of fishes

       Flying. The rite is shorn
Of nightingale and centaur dead horse. The springs wither
Back. Lines of age sleep on the stones till trumpeting dawn.
Exultation lies down. Time buries the spring weather
That belled and bounded with the fossil and the dew
    reborn.

       For the bird lay bedded
In a choir of wings, as though she slept or died,
And the wings glided wide and he was hymned and
    wedded,

And through the thighs of the engulfing bride,
The woman breasted and the heaven headed

      Bird, he was brought low,
Burning in the bride bed of love, in the whirl-
Pool at the wanting centre, in the folds
Of paradise, in the spun bud of the world.
And she rose with him flowering in her melting snow.

c. 1946   DYLAN THOMAS

Encounter

A mist fell,
And without warning a door swung open;
I stood naked between mountains.
There was nothing in my hands,
My lips were bloodless, my tongue
Had forgotten its language.
No sounds were in this place,
Nor shadows,
Only an endless avenue of needle rocks
And a beetle burrowing among bones.

A black cloud lowered
As I began my journey down the corridor,
Treading the while on sharp stones,
Shards, and the brooches of former travellers;
There were abandoned helmets there, broken axles,
And some old rusted guns,
A shattered hour glass,
And the ruins of vulture's wings.
And in a crevice, water played
Without an echo round the diadems of kings;

His eyes half stopped with dust,
A grey moth settled on an iron flower.

I came out into a great plain,
Without horizons or any vegetation,
A kind of long, colourless glacier
That seemed to have known no living thing,
Almost suspended between the void and creation;
This region had never heard laughter,
Nor tides,
Nor wind.

And then I halted
On the track that separated
One silence from another;
A figure in the terrible distance moved towards me
As relentlessly as day advances upon night,
Nearer it came and slower I
Went out to meet it.

It was myself.

c. 1948   LEONARD CLARK

The Moment

To write down all I contain at this moment
I would pour the desert through an hour-glass,
The sea through a water-clock,
Grain by grain and drop by drop
Let in the trackless, measureless, mutable seas and sands.

For earth's days and nights are breaking over me
The tides and sands are running through me,

And I have only two hands and a heart to hold the
    desert and the sea.

What can I contain of it? It escapes and eludes me
The tides wash me away
The desert shifts under my feet.

c. 1946   KATHLEEN RAINE

The Changing Wind

Past my window runs a tree,
All the leaves are in my room,
A shiver of water passes over.
There is no stillness ever again.

I saw the table break in three,
I saw the walls cascading down,
I saw the hard hair of my lover
Drift out upon the flowing green.
I saw the clove dark enemy
Stare from the bed where I had lain,
I saw my face in hers to be.
There is no stillness ever again.

Sun and wind had come for me –
What is my house but a flight of wings?
A flight of leaves, a flutter of rain,
A sidelong slipping of light in rings?

And now a scream possesses me –
Too high to hear, yet can I hear it;
And now transfixed upon a pain,

Too thin to feel yet must I bear it.
– This scream, this pain, they are not mine,
Water and air is all I am,
A tree has shaken the staircase down –
Then what has rustled and entered in?

I knew the other ones had come.
I knew my heart was theirs to claim.
I felt the millions in my room.
There is no being alone again.

p. 1946   JULIAN ORDE

Air

Element that utters doves, angels and cleft flames,
The bees of Helicon and the cloudy houses,
Impulse of music and the word's equipoise,

Dancer that never wearies of the dance
That prints in the blown dust eternal wisdom
Or carves its abstract sculptures in the snow,
The wind unhindered passes beyond its trace.

But from a high fell on a summer day
Sometimes below you may see the air like water,
The dazzle of the light upon its waves
That flow unbroken to the bend of the world.

The bird of god descends between two moments
Like silence into music, opening a way through time.

c. 1949   KATHLEEN RAINE

The Seed

I am the small million.
I am the locked fountain.

Late, late, in summer's dotage
When they stand gaunt and blasted,
The hollyhock tower and the cottage
Of clover, and age has wasted
The sun – then, then at last
I jump, I glide, a waif
Victoriously lost,
Tempestuously safe.

I go as weak as sea-water.
I lie as quiet as radium.

In the dust-high caravan, in
The cabin of a bird's claw,
Or sheepback I travel, I have been
In the whale, his prophesying maw;
I have occupied both town
And parish, an airborne spirit, a
Soldier in thistledown,
A meek inheritor.

I am dry but I shall slake you.
I am hard but I shall satisfy you.

The apple contains me and I
Contain the apple, I balance
A field on a stalk and tie
A century's voices in silence;

And all the hopes of the happy
And all the sighs of the sorry
Rest in my power to copy
And copying vary.

I am the first omega.
I am the last alpha.

And remember, I lie beneath
All soils of time, fears' frost;
Remember, I stir in my death,
Most missed I am least lost;
Remember, in the gaunt garden
In the kingdom of a broken tree
You will find after Armageddon,
After the deluge, me.

p. 1948   HAL SUMMERS

Woman to Lover

I am fire
Stilled to water,

A wave
Lifting from the abyss.

In my veins
The moon-drawn tide rises
Into a tree of flowers
Scattered in sea-foam.

I am air,
Caught in a net,

The prophetic bird
That sings in a reflected sky,

I am a dream before nothingness,
I am a crown of stars,
I am the way to die.

c. 1949   KATHLEEN RAINE

The Wall

The place where our two gardens meet
Is undivided by a street,
And mingled flower and weed caress
And fill our double wilderness,
Among whose riot undismayed
And unreproached, we idly played,
While, unaccompanied by fears,
The months extended into years,
Till we went down one day in June
To pass the usual afternoon
And there discovered, shoulder-tall,
Rise in the wilderness a wall:
The wall which put us out of reach
And into silence split our speech.
We knew, and we had always known
That some dark, unseen hand of stone
Hovered across our days of ease,
And strummed its tunes upon the breeze.
It had not tried us overmuch,
But here it was, for us to touch.

The wilderness is still as wild,

And separately unreconciled
The tangled thickets play and sprawl
Beneath the shadows of our wall,
And the wall varies with the flowers
And has its seasons and its hours.
Look at its features wintrily
Frozen to transparency;
Through it an icy music swells
And a brittle, brilliant chime of bells:
Would you conjecture that, in Spring,
We lean upon it, talk and sing,
Or climb upon it, and play chess
Upon its summer silentness?
One certain thing alone we know:
Silence or song, it does not go.
A habit now to wake with day
And watch it catch the sun's first ray,
Or terrorized, to scramble through
The depths of night to prove it true.

We need not doubt, for such a wall
Is based in death, and does not fall.

c. 1946   HENRY REED

Three Pleas

Stand by me, Death, lest these dark days
Should hurt me more than I may know;
I beg that if the wound grows sharp
You take me when I ask to go.

Step closer, Love, and dry your eyes,
What's marred you'll never mend by tears;

206

Let's finish where the tale began
And kiss away the ruined years.

A moment, Faith, before you leave,
There's one last favour I would ask;
Put to some use your handsome hand
And show me the face behind your mask.

p. 1943   HENRY TREECE

The Divided Ways

(IN MEMORY OF SIDNEY KEYES)

He has gone down into the dark cellar
To talk with the bright-faced Spirit with silver hair;
But I shall never know what word was spoken there.

. . . . .

My friend is out of earshot. Our ways divided
Before we even knew we had missed each other.
For he advanced
Into a stony wilderness of the heart,
Under a hostile and a red-clawed sun;
All that dry day, until the darkness fell,
I heard him going, and shouting among the canyons.
But I, struck backward from the eastern gate,
Had turned aside, obscure,
Beneath the unfriendly silence of the moon,
My long white fingers on a small carved lute.
There was a forest, and faces known in childhood
Rose unexpected from the mirrored pools;
The trees had hands to clutch my velvet shoulders,
And birds of fever sang among the branches;

207

Till the dark vine-boughs, breaking as I seized them,
And dripping blood, cried out with my own voice:
'I also have known thirst, and the wanderer's terror! . . .'
But I had lost my friend and the mountain paths;
And if there might have been another meeting –
The new sun rising in a different sky,
Having repaired his light in the streams of Ocean,
And the moon, white and maternal, going down
Over the virgin hills – it is too late
Ever to find it now.

And though it was in May that the reptile guns
And breeze-fly bullets took my friend away,
It is no time to forge a delicate idyll
Of the young shepherd, stricken, prone among
The flowers of spring, heavy with morning dew,
And emblematic blood of dying gods;
Or that head pillowed on a wave's white fleece,
Softly drowning in a Celtic sea.
This was more harsh and meaningless than winter.

But now, at last, I dare avow my terror
Of the pale vampire by the cooling grate;
The enemy face that doubled every loved one;
My secret fear of him and his cold heroes;
The meaning of the dream
Which was so fraught with trouble for us both;
And how through this long autumn
(Sick and tempestuous with another sorrow)
His spirit, vexed, fluttered among my thoughts,
A bird returning to the darkened window –
The hard-eyed albatross with scissor bill.
And I would ask his pardon for this weakness.

But he is gone where no hallooing voice
Nor beckoning hand can ever call him back;

And what is ours of him
Must speak impartially for all the world;
There is no personal word remains for me,
And I pretend to find no meaning here.
Though I might guess that other Singer's wisdom
Who saw in Death a dark immaculate flower,
And tenderness in every falling autumn,
This abstract music will not bring again
My friend to his warm room:
Inscrutable the darkness covers him.

c. 1946   JOHN HEATH-STUBBS

On a Dying Boy

Oh leave his body broken on the rocks
where fainting sense may drown beneath the sound
of the complaining surf. His spirit mocks
our ignorant attempts to hem it round:
as eagerly as body sought the ground
into its native ocean must it flow.
Oh let his body lie where it was found,
there's nothing we can do to help him now.

And hide his face under his tattered coat
until the women come to where he lies,
they come to bind the silence in his throat
and shut the eternal darkness in his eyes,
to wash the cold sweat of his agonies
and wash the blood that's clotted on his brow.
Cover his face from the unfriendly skies,
there's nothing we can do to help him now.

And watch even his enemies forget him,
the skies forget his sobs, the rocks his blood:

and think how neither rock nor sky dared let him
grow old enough for evil or for good;
and then forget him too. Even if we could
bring back the flower that's fallen from the bough,
bring back the flower that never left the bud,
there's nothing we can do to help him now.

c. 1950   WILLIAM BELL

The Wedding

Because there was no moon
our young sister was married
by the light of the stars.
She walked slowly the length
of the aisle of the river,
the stones arched above her
and the windows were water
patterned with lilies and garlands
    of reeds.
She walked with her bridegroom
down the nave of the sea
to the peal of the waves
and lightly-flung sand grains.
We called to her, called to her
and the echo returned to us
from the vaults of the ocean.
Because there was no moon
our young sister was married
by the light of the stars
and her heart was closed
within a light ring of coral.

p. 1947   ROLAND GANT

Drowned Man

You naked-shouldered sea-waves, you who are
Eternally choral round the jag-toothed shore,
Rend from the stone the sucker-footed wrack,
The many-bubbled weed from the rock's core.

How have I seen you, herded in the West,
Towards the evening moaning as you run,
Your iron-throated bells still heralding
In pain and crimson sacrificed, the sun!

And oh, among what depths, by what weeds tangled,
Wanders the proud sea-skimmer, shambles the drowned
Boy cut at by oyster-shells, and his limbs mangled,
His body laid where your cold requiems sound?

What peace has he, when jewelled fishes come
To strip the flesh from his well-moulded bones?
Only unending pain, while the tides roll
Him round and round among the glittering stones.

Colder than fishes' eyes, his eyes are crushed
By weight of many waters from his head,
But all his dead flesh sees grass-green, grass-green,
And fields that torture the remembering Dead.

Grass-green of fields – and in the Spring his girl
Said she would wait for him. Last Spring – but now
Are other honeyed kisses! O drowned man
Hang up your heart upon the coral bough!

And nevermore down to this salt-paved deep
To sponge or weed may change of seasons come

Nor even the sea-birds' crying, but the beat
Of monstrous bat-like things whose throats are dumb.

O measureless foam-crested pitiless
And cruel-fronted purity of the wave
Drag down the weakness of young flesh, and wring
Your smarting tears over his sand-smudged grave.

c. 1943   JOHN HEATH-STUBBS

Griefs of the Sea

It is fitting to mourn dead sailors,
To crown the sea with some wild wreath of foam
On some steep promontory, some cornercliff of Wales
Though the deaf wave hear nothing.

It is fitting to fling off clothing,
To enter the sea with plunge of seawreaths white
Broken by limbs that love the waters, fear the stars,
Though the blind wave grope under eyes that see, limbs
   that wonder,
Though the blind wave grope forward to the sand
With a greedy, silvered hand.

It is a horrible sound, the low wind's whistle
Across the seaweeds on the beach at night.
From stone to stone through hissing caves it passes
Up the curved cliff and shakes the prickly thistle
And spreads its hatred through the grasses.

In spite of that wicked sound
Of the wind that follows us like a scenting hound,
It is fitting on the curved cliff to remember the drowned,

To imagine them clearly for whom the sea no longer cares,
To deny the language of the thistle, to meet their
    foot-firm tread
Across the dark-sown tares
Who were skilful and erect, magnificent types of godhead,
To resist the dogging wind, to accuse the sea-god;
Yet in that gesture of anger we must admit
We were quarrelling with a phantom unawares.

For the sea turns whose every drop is counted
And the sand turns whose every grain a holy hour-glass
    holds
And the weeds turn beneath the sea, the sifted life slips
    free,
And the wave turns surrendering from its folds
All things that are not sea, and thrown off is the spirit
By the sea, the riderless horse which they once mounted.

c. 1941   VERNON WATKINS

Men Sign the Sea

Men sign the sea.
One warbreath more sucked round the roaring veins
Keeping the heart in ark then down loud mountains
After his cry.

This that the sea
Moves through moves over sea-tongued the whole waters
Woven over their breath. So can the floating fires
Blow down on any.

This deep time, scaling broadside the cannoning sea,
Tilting, cast rigged among galloping iron vesselwork,

Snapped wirerope, spitting oil, steam screamed out jets,
Bomb drunkard hero herded by the hammerheaded
    elements,
Loud raftered foamfloored house, a waved scorched hand
Over final upheaval and the decked combers.
The filling limpet shell's slow gyre round the drowned.
The cairns of foam stand up. The signed sea flowers.

The love-signed sea
Weeded with words and branched with human ores
Lights up. An arm waves off the land. Thunderous
Time mines the sea.

Men sign the sea,
Maintained on memory's emerald over the drowned.
This that the sea moves through drives through the land
Twin to their cry.

c. 1949   W. S. GRAHAM

News of the World III

Let her lie naked here, my hand resting
Light on her broken breast, the sleeping world
Given into our far from careful keeping,
Terrestrial daughter of a disaster of waters
No master honours. Let her lie tonight
Attended by those visions of bright swords
That never defended but ended life.
My emerald trembler, my sky skipping scullion,
See, now, your sister, dipping into the horizon,
Leaves us in darkness; you, nude, and I
Seeking to loose what the day retrieves,
An immoderation of love. Bend your arm

214

Under my generation of heads. The seas enfold
My sleepless eye and save it weeping
For the dishonoured star. I hear your grave
Nocturnal lamentation, where, abandoned, far,
You, like Arabia in her tent, mourn through an evening
Of wildernesses. O what are you grieving for?
From the tiara'd palaces of the Andes
And the last Asiatic terraces, I see
The wringing of the hands of all of the world,
I hear your long lingering of disillusion.
Favour the viper, heaven, with one vision
That it may see what is lost. The crime is blended
With the time and the cause. But at your
Guilty and golden bosom, O daughter of laws,
I happy lie tonight, the fingering zephyr
Light and unlikely as a kiss. The shades creep
Out of their holes and graves for a last
Long look at your bare empire as it rolls
Its derelict glory away into darkness. Turn, liar,
Back. Our fate is in your face. Whom do you love
But those whom you doom to the happy disgrace
Of adoring you with degradations? I garb my wife,
The wide world of a bride, in devastations.
She has curled up in my hand, and, like a moth,
Died a legend of splendour along the line of my life.
But the congregation of clouds paces in dolour
Over my head and her never barren belly
Where we lie, summered, together, a world and I.
Her birdflecked hair, sunsetting the weather,
Feathers my eye, she shakes an ear-ring sky,
And her hand of a country trembles against me.
The glittering nightriders gambol through
A zodiac of symbols above our love
Promising, O my star-crossed, death and disasters.
But I want breath for nothing but your possession

Now, now, this summer midnight, before the dawn
Shakes its bright gun in the sky, before
The serried battalions of lies and organizations of hate
Entirely encompass us, buried; before the wolf and friend
Render us enemies. Before all this,
Lie one night in my arms and give me peace.

c. 1950   GEORGE BARKER

'NOW THERE IS NOTHING
NEW...'

The Civilization

By their frock-coated leaders,
By the frequency of their wars,
By the depth of their hunger,
Their numberless refugees,
And the brevity of their verse,
They were distinguished.

Their revolutions
Were thwarted by kisses.
The cold mathematicians
Aged into blurred philosophers.
Their poets choked on
The parallel of past calamities.

Their funeral customs, art,
Physique, and secret
Societies, unequal:
Their doom inevitable.
Ambiguous as dreams
Their symbolic poetry.

Yes, it had happened
Before. Ill-pictured leaders,
Food-queues in foodless places,
Migration to areas
Of moderate terror,
Monotonous poems.

Then horses galloping
Over burned foundations,
Ascetic communities,
The improbable moon,

Death from a cut,
Bleak, eroded spaces;

And eventually the strangers,
With the luxury of spices,
Effective weapons,
Their tales of travel,
Their ikons of leaders,
Their epic verse.

c. 1949   ROY FULLER

Aftermath

The apple-blossom in the sky,
The old tin cans left in the ditch
Alone remain now to bewitch
The tired memory's purblind eye.

Sometimes a vagrant scent recalls
The smell of cordite in the rain,
And suddenly the penny falls
Into its slot to start again

The mechanism of the mind:
Kaleidoscopic pictures clear
Of incidents that were assigned
Deliberately to death appear

To haunt the golden light of day.
The awful stillness of the hand
Protruding from the blanket grey,
The eyes of those who understand

What night will bring, of those who see
That life is balanced on the thread
Of chance that will be certainty
When their small stock of hope has fled.

Yet soon the power that drives the mind
Is spent and then the pictures pall,
And there is peace until that blind
Fool Fortune lets a penny fall.

c. 1948   VERNON SCANNELL

The Chief Stoker's Song

Time and Space and History,
– all the brainy school-kids know
a man who writes Philosophy
had rubbed their faces in the muck.
(And a hundred years ago
none of us had given a damn.)

Time fell ill, and Time has died.
The Gunner topples to and fro,
the Bo'sun sways from side to side
like a bloody weathercock,
(and a hundred years ago
the taverns shut at ten o'clock.)

Expanding Space unrolls her chart.
On Pompey Hard and Plymouth Hoe
Jolly Jack walks with his tart
or lies beside his bit of fluff,
(and a hundred years ago
those benches were not long enough.)

A blowsy bitch is History
who will not let her friends forget her:
what's she ever done for me?
Turning out is still a curse,
nothing changes for the better
and the beer is getting worse.

c. 1950   WILLIAM BELL

From the Notebook of a European Tramp

XI

The townsman on his yielding bed
thinks that the world will end when he
on the bare floor-boards lies instead.
He also who was forced to see
the mind's own mattresses ripped up
and many a recipient head
smashed like a saucer or a cup
feels that by rights he should be dead.

True, there are moments when he finds
that metaphysics was no more
than luxury of idle minds,
soft padding round a rotten core –
particularly in the spring
when Chaos, ever young, unbinds
gods who are game for anything
and demi-gods of various kinds.

In winter, though, he's far from sure:
he says his prayers just in case
a word in the right place might cure
his pangs, redeem all men's disgrace;

222

and still it seems a little weird
that the earth's axle is secure
when all the nightmares he most feared
prosper in daylight and endure.

1945 or 1946
c. 1950   MICHAEL HAMBURGER

Virtue

In these old hackneyed melodïes
Hollow in the piano's cage
I see the whole trash of the age –
      Art, gadgets, bombs and lies.

Such tunes can move me to confess
The trash moves, too: that what offends
Or kills can in its simplest ends,
      Being human, also bless.

c. 1949   ROY FULLER

Pub

The glasses are raised, the voices drift into laughter,
The clock hands have stopped, the beer in the hands of
   the soldiers
Is blond, the faces are calm and the fingers can feel
The wet touch of glasses, the glasses print rings on
   the table,
The smoke rings curl and go up and dissolve near the
   ceiling,
         This moment exists and is real.

223

What is reality? Do not ask that. At this moment
Look at the butterfly eyes of the girls, watch the
    barmaid's
Precision in pouring a Scotch, and remember this day,
This day at this moment you were no longer an island,
People were friendly, the clock in the hands of the
    soldiers
           For this moment had nothing to say.

And nothing to say and the glasses are raised, we are
    happy
Drinking through time, and a world that is gentle and
    helpless
Survives in the pub and goes up in the smoke of our
    breath,
The regulars doze in the corner, the talkers are fluent;
Look now in the faces of those you love and remember
           That you are not thinking of death.

But thinking of death as the lights go out and the glasses
Are lowered, the people go out, and the evening
Goes out, ah, goes out like a light and leaves you alone,
As the heart goes out, the door opens out into darkness,
The foot takes a step, and the moment, the moment of
    falling
           Is here, you go down like a stone.

Are you able to meet the disaster, able to meet the
Cold air of the street and the touch of corruption, the
    rotting
Fingers that murder your own in the grip of love?
Can you bear to find hateful the faces you once thought
    were lovely,
Can you bear to find comfort alone in the evil and
    stunted,
           Can you bear to abandon the dove?

The houses are shut and the people go home, we are
  left in
Our islands of pain, the clocks start to move and the
  powerful
To act, there is nothing now, nothing at all
To be done: for the trouble is real: and the verdict is
  final
Against us. The clocks go round faster and faster. And
  fast as confetti
      The days are beginning to fall.

p. 1942   JULIAN SYMONS

Ideas of Disorder at Torquay

I

The trams still run in some kind of array,
Along the seafront with its curled white foam
And reminiscent gardens on the rocks,
Goldenrod, saxifrage, imperious lupins
Waving a kind of welcome to the sea:
The trams still run against the times' dismay,
Leaving an old-world order in Torquay.

II

And there the aunts sit with their gorgeous knitting,
Watching the children's kites high in the bay:
The needles go click-click against the sky,
The cloud and sunshine, and the rocking sea,
The flowers and the nurses. In the bay
The little steamers puff their purple smoke
As if to say order in everything.

III

And the hotels on the majestic front
Fill up with visitors, old, ancient ladies,
And proud magnates from factory and bank.
In the ballrooms they hum God-save-the-King,
Among the flowery asters and the dark . . .
Dun dowagers with breasts of precious pearl,
Lords and ladies out of a distant world.

IV

Meanwhile the vulgar in their hordes disdain
The imperial order, and the rabble ride
Upon what trains they can to Blackpool Pier,
To look for lights they used to know. Click-click,
The Torquay needles clack to help the troops,
While what wild engineers grab Blackpool buns,
Hoping to find an old-world holiday.

V

Such reading sends a shudder of disgust . . .
As who would not, among lupins and roses,
Watching the quiet foam of Devon water,
And doing duty with wound reams of wool,
Contemplating disorder. . . . Who would not
Protest that such order might be destroyed?
The same thrilling distaste runs through the roses,
As cold disaster in detective stories.

VI

And murmurs heave the quiet, contented ladies,
Whose withered bosoms hold bright emerald jewels,

As if to say the young are so, so strange,
As if to say the world was in its ruins,
With such experiments, with such wild fancies,
The Russian fantasy. And edibles
Run out because of war, and chew on grief
Becomes the order of the day, old ladies.

VII

The trams still run. In the white-ribbed café,
It is still possible to take coffee,
Or in the gorgeous flower-perfect lounge
Sip gentle teas. Order is possible.
The lupins and the saxifrage have it.
So does the welcoming and battling sea,
The gentle rocks. But something holds dismay
Like a round moon upon faded Torquay.
Something, the essence of a change that seems
A breaking up of order, something grave
Troubles the waters of contentment, moves
The old, cold ladies to a troubled love.

c. 1942   NICHOLAS MOORE

The Photographs

The faces in the obscene photographs
Look out with no expression: they are like
The dead, who always look as though surprised
In a most intimate attitude. The man
And woman in the photographs have faces
Of corpses; their positions are of love, –
Which you and I have taken. These

Images haunt me: I remember how
Once coming from the sea I slipped the *maillot*,
While we were standing in the sun-warmed house,
And found your bosom soft and round and cold:
And on this memory is now imposed
The phantasies engendered by these two.

Before me in the evening an aircraft
Is speckled with tiny brown and crimson birds;
The plain extends to an escarpment which
Is lit by the curtained sun as by a candle;
And then there is the great curve of the earth
And, after, you, whom two oceans and a war
Divides.
      The air is full of dust: the land
And sky are enormous, bored with narrow tunnels
Down which I crawl. As long as those eternal
Photographs gnaw my imagination
I shall not dare to catch my countenance
In any mirror; for it seems to me
Our faces, bodies – both of us – are dead.

c. 1944   ROY FULLER

The Clock

Midnight: and the familiar books stand
Suave under glass or open to the hand:
    Only the clock says *Have you ever been happy?*

The minutes pass and the thick books say
The question each asks each is the best way:
    Only the clock says *Is the answer truthful?*

The minutes pass and these slow words climb
Into the single gesture of a rhyme:
    Only the clock says *Your wishes are not simple.*

The books and rhyme are done, the mind goes
To peace in dreams, the restless heart flows
Down to the natural quiet of dog and rose:
    Only the clock says *Morning will bring no comfort.*

c. 1943   JULIAN SYMONS

Detective Story

The stranger left the house in the small hours;
A neighbour heard his steps between two dreams;
The body was discovered strewn with flowers;
Their evenings were too passionate, it seems.

They used to be together quite a lot;
The friend was dressed in black, distinguished looking
The porter said; his wife had always thought
They were so nice and interested in cooking.

And this was true perhaps. The other night
They made a soup that was a great success;
They drank some lager too and all was right,
The talk, the kisses and at last the chess.

'It was great fun!' they said; yet their true love
Throbbed in their breasts like pus that must be freed.
The porter found the weapon and the glove,
But only our despair can find the creed.

c. 1947   DEMETRIOS CAPETANAKIS

The Carcase

This carcase still survives
For, see, it keeps its teeth,
The furious maggot thrives;
But we who walk the heath,
Devoid of all but breath,
Bear in our murdered lives
A deadlier kind of death.

Victim of trap or gun
The rabbit triumphs still
And all's again begun.
But we who hourly kill
Each other without blow
See nothing good or ill
From that corruption grow.

This is in truth to die
When all men do or say,
Love, hate and apathy,
Consume and fall away,
Leaving no other need
Their dying wills betray
Except that they be freed.

p. 1949   FRANCIS KING

Nocturnal III

Now the night lays ghostly charms
in the lover's anxious arms,
and his hapless dreams devise
whispering, the familiar lies
as the futile and the great
go their ways by the same gate.

Formless hands and shadowless
mock us in our meek distress;
one by one nostalgic feet
tread the lonely rainy street;
images of easy tears
follow the false comforters.

Now the trains run roaring through
a hollow sky from me to you,
and destructive resonant things
cross the moon on rigid wings:
but the bridge is broken down
and the homeward signal gone.

Arms outstretched across the bay
lift the lovely hill of day,
but the lover's arms are spread
vainly in his haunted bed.
Time puts out a hand to break
the hearts of them that dare not wake.

c. 1941   TERENCE TILLER

Out of Sleep

Surfacing out of sleep she feared
voices in the sky talking
with thick tongues. Night flashed
brightening her eyelids; Yet as panic cleared
she knew those voices never spoke the harsh
brogue of the guns; And then the rain
sighed in the leaves; it was thunder.
The rain said, hush.

It has been peace in our world a year:
What worse-than-memories seep
to infect our nights with fear
up from the angers of that other war,
ours copy here?
What towns burn on what darker coast of sleep,
how many histories deep?

p. 1947   BERNARD SPENCER

A Great Unhealthy Friendship

There was a great unhealthy friendship
Developed in a stark old district
Between a student and a God
Who languishing in opposite lodgings
Signalled across the street their greetings
And cared not whither it might lead.

At tables outside costly cafés
Or visiting asylums' inmates

232

They found they had too much in common
Till all each others' books were finished
Till they had slept each other silly
Till mind on mind preyed like the ichneumon.

The God departed without paying
And ever after human-shunning
Donned an impenetrable disguise.
The student took life like harmless poison
And never met a normal person
And won renown for formal views.

1942   DRUMMOND ALLISON
c. 1944

The Man in the Bowler Hat

I am the unnoticed, the unnoticeable man:
The man who sat on your right in the morning train:
The man you looked through like a windowpane:
The man who was the colour of the carriage, the colour
  of the mounting
Morning pipe smoke.

I am the man too busy with a living to live,
Too hurried and worried to see and smell and touch:
The man who is patient too long and obeys too much
And wishes too softly and seldom.

I am the man they call the nation's backbone,
Who am boneless – playable catgut, pliable clay:
The Man they label Little lest one day
I dare to grow.

233

I am the rails on which the moment passes,
The megaphone for many words and voices:
I am graph, diagram,
Composite face.

I am the led, the easily-fed,
The tool, the not-quite-fool,
The would-be-safe-and-sound,
The uncomplaining bound,
The dust fine-ground,
Stone-for-a-statue waveworn pebble-round.

c. 1947   A. S. J. TESSIMOND

Departure Platform

Always to look like this
At the unmeeting place:
Scrambling of crowds and air
When the gilt clock-hands move
Across the wet moon-face
(Seen, cheek touching lip,
Through your distracting hair)
To enter time again
Where disappointments live
In shabby comradeship.

All this is nothing new

Still on the stroke of four
A wilderness of rail
Into which we have come
Feeling like all the lost
Ten tribes of Israel,

234

Maybe to see and hear
The hobbled tree of steam
Lofting between the wheels
Its paradisal hiss
Under a dripping roof;

The rain still falling now

To share a jealous dream
Of pert and slithering heels
In the rain's puddled glass,
Who have the time I leave,
And all the afternoon
A bitter nail, a clove,
A high, blind window pane
When the black pistons drive
Where but away from love.

Now there is nothing new

p. 1947   KENNETH ALLOTT

Express

As the through-train of words with white-hot whistle
Shrills past the heart's mean halts, the mind's full stops,
With all the signals down; past the small town
Contentment, and the citizens all leaning
And loitering parenthetically
In waiting-rooms, or interrogative on platforms;
Its screaming mouth crammed tight with urgent meaning,
– I, by it borne on, look out and wonder
To what happy or calamitous terminus
I am bound, what anonymity or what renown.

O if at length into Age, the last of all stations,
It slides and slows, and its smoky mane of thunder
Thins out, and I detrain; when I stand in that place
On whose piers and wharves, from all sources and seas,
Men wearily arrive – I pray that still
I may have with me my pities and indignations.

c. 1941   W. R. RODGERS

The Sleeping Passenger

The train relinquishes the station,
The doors slap shut, the posters slide,
And the windows move, in green gradation,
On to opening fans of countryside
Whose revolutions intrude no shape
Into your sleep's untroubled void.

Your father begot you in his sleep
– And your mother was probably sleeping too.
You have never wakened up,
Even when your eyes open blue
Windows of astonishment
Into a world they do not know,
They see it as an awkward instant
– A something not to be inquired into.

Though all should founder – or at least shake,
You ripen like fruit on a sunny wall,
Too cosy asleep ever to wake:
Waiting to be picked, or to fall.
Your untroubled blood dictates
Growth asleep, like a vegetable.

You are unacquainted with the fates,
For you there is no precipice
Between this state and other states.
What was, what will be, and what is
Indistinguishably harden
Into the rails whose rhythm marries
Your dream to its mechanical burden.

You do not talk of the atom bomb,
The weather, or what grows in your garden.
Unbothered by daily news or doom
You have taken conscience and let it slip
Back to the limbo where it came from.
Others may be puzzled, you can cope,
You are master of your situation
Because you have never sized it up.
You have already reached your destination.

p. 1946   DAVID PAUL

A Vagrant

'*Mais il n'a point parlé, mais cette année encore
Heure par heure en vain lentement tombera.*'
                                        Alfred de Vigny

'They're much the same in most ways, these great cities.
  Of them all,
Speaking of those I've seen, this one's still far the best
Big densely built-up area for a man to wander in
Should he have ceased to find shelter, relief,
Or dream in sanatorium bed; should nothing as yet call
Decisively to him to put an end to brain's
Proliferations round the possibilities that eat
Up adolescence, even years up to the late
Thirtieth birthday; should no-one seem to wait

237

His coming, to pop out at last and bark
Briskly: "A most convenient solution has at last
Been found, after the unavoidable delay due to this
    spate of wars
That we've been having lately. This is it:
Just fill in (in block letters) on the dotted-line your name
And number. From now on until you die all is
O.K., meaning the clockwork's been adjusted to
    accommodate
You nicely; all you need's to eat and sleep,
To sleep and eat and eat and laugh and sleep,
And sleep and laugh and wake up every day
Fresh as a raffia daisy!" I already wake each day
Without a bump or too much morning sickness to routine
Which although without order wears the will out just
    as well
As this job-barker's programme would. His line may in
    the end
Provide me with a noose with which to hang myself,
    should I
Discover that the strain of doing nothing is too great
A price to pay for spiritual integrity. The soul
Is said by some to be a bourgeois luxury, which shows
A strange misunderstanding both of soul and bourgeoisie.
The Sermon on the Mount is just as often misconstrued
By Marxists as by wealthy congregations, it would seem.
The "Modern Man in Search of Soul" appears
A comic criminal or an unbalanced bore to those
Whose fear of doing something foolish fools them. *Je*
    m'en fous!
Blessèd are they, it might be said, who are not of this
    race
Of settled average citizens secure in their *état*
Civil of snowy guiltlessness and showy high ideals
Permitting them achieve an inexpensive lifelong peace

Of mind, through dogged persistence, frequent aspirin,
   and bile
Occasionally vented via trivial slander . . . Baa,
Baa, O sleepysickness-rotted sheep, in your nice fold
Are none but marketable fleeces. I my lot
Prefer to cast at once away right in
Among the stone-winning lone wolves whose future cells
Shall make home-founding unworthwhile. Unblessèd
   let me go
And join the honest tribe of patient prisoners and ex-
Convicts, and all such victims of the guilt
Society dare not admit its own. I would not strike
The pose of one however who might in a chic ballet
Perform an apache role in rags of cleverly-cut silk.
Awkward enough, awake, yet although anxious still
   just sane,
I stand still in my quasi-dereliction, or but stray
Slowly along the quais towards the ends of afternoons
That lead to evenings empty of engagements, or at night
Lying resigned in cosy-corner crow's nest, listen long
To sounds of the surrounding city desultorily
Seeking in loud distraction some relief from what its
   nerves
Are gnawed by: I mean knowledge of its lack of *raison
   d'être*.
The city's lack and mine are much the same. What, oh
   what can
A vagrant hope to find to take the place of what was once
Our expectation of the Human City, in which each man
   might
Morning and evening, every day, lead his own life, and
   Man's?'

Spring 1948   DAVID GASCOYNE
p. 1948

1950

Elegy for a Dead God

Leave us alone. Leave us, hope
of our deliverance, leave us alone.
We did not deserve
the wonder in our midst,
for by inexcusable error
that we knew, and did not
know we were committing,
we ignored his nature and his need.

Give us a dead flower, O someone,
a dead leaf, a glass wreath,
give us the telescoping spine
of dim and dimmer-focussed dying,
the crack of the dead branch
torn by the gale of earth
from the air's crashing tree,
the shot hare's human crying.

What is our fault, what word
did we utter as if it were untrue?
Give us a dead bird
in the broken nest of our clasping fingers
And let it lie there
under the dead thought of our speaking,
under the dry lips of our inconsolable
weeping, under the dead fright of our eyes.

Wandering all night in the forgotten rain,
we did not know, we knew too well that impermanent
divinity, but all we could think of was the tall
presence inhabiting our loneliness.
Now voices in the afternoon calling from across the
    street

are always yours, and yours the steps running towards us
at evening, to greet our solitude with words and wishes,
measuring the depths of heaven with a light remark.

Why did you ever speak to us,
O, why did you let us drink
the wines we did not know,
and now will never know?
Why did you teach us smiles
that were not our own, and strange
laughter that we loved, and a loquacity
rich and curious to our startled throats?

For we are an ignorant people: not
omniscient, because we know too much.
What was it killed you?
What careless look, meaningless clutch
of dying hands towards the never-dying,
what unspoken tenderness too much
in our unbroken silences? And yet,
what god were you, who did not understand our
    sentences?

Love begets love, so they said.
It was not love that begot ours,
and the love we had for you
destroyed you with its cruelty.
What is the meaning of this song without you?
What is love, now that it fails its own believers?
Only forgive our blindness, and your pain,
forgive your knowledge of our pain.

Dead to us, you cannot die.
And when we, lost ones,
wander in your city's emptiness,

you are everywhere and nowhere, as a god should be.
But we grow sick with memories, cannot forget the
   shadow at our sides
that is the only remnant of the air you took away.
Be comforted, remembering the forsaken faces of the dead
who once knew love that touched to life
the stilled darkness at the centre of the smallest stone.
For though you were a god, we know that you, too, are
   much alone.

p. 1950   JAMES KIRKUP

Channel Crossing

And just by crossing the short sea
To find the answer sitting there
Combing out its snakey hair
And with a smile regarding me
Because it knows only too well
That I shall never recognize
The verities that I should prize
And the lies that I should tell.

I saw the question in the sky
Ride like a gull to fool me, as
The squat boat butted at the seas
As grossly as through mysteries I
Churn up a frothy wake of verbs
Or stir a muddy residue
Looking for the answer who
Sanctifies as she disturbs.

The horror of the question-mark
Looking back I saw stand over

The white and open page of Dover
Huge as the horn of the scapegoat. Dark
It stood up in the English day
Interrogating Destiny
With the sad lip of the sea:
'What can a dead nation say?'

As these words wailed in the air
I looked at Europe and I saw
The glittering instruments of war
Grow paler but not go from where
Like a livid sunset on
The marble of the horizon
They lay foretelling for tomorrow
Another day of human sorrow.

But when I turned and looked into
The silent chambers of the sea
I saw the displaced fishes flee
From nowhere into nowhere through
Their continent of liberty.
O skipping porpoise of the tide
No longer shall the sailors ride
You cheering out to sea.

I thought of Britain in its cloud
Chained to the economic rocks
Dying behind me; saw the flocks
Of great and grieving omens crowd
About the lion on the stone;
I heard Milton's eagle mewing
Her dereliction in the ruin
Of a great nation alone.

That granite and gigantic sigh

Of the proud man beaten by
Those victories from which we die;
The gentle and defeated grief
Of the gale that moans among
Trees that are a day too strong
And, victorious by a leaf,
Show the winner he was wrong.

The continent of discontent
Rose up before me as I stood
Above the happy fish. Endued
With hotter and unhappier blood,
Contented in my discontent,
I saw that every man's a soul
Caught in a glass wishing bowl:
To live at peace in discontent.

O somewhere in the seven leagues
That separate us from the stricken
Amphitheatre of the spirit,
O somewhere in that baleful sea
The answer to sad Europe lodges,
The clue that causes us to sicken
Because we cannot find and share it,
Or, finding, cannot see.

So in the sky, the monstrous sun
Mocked like a punishment to be,
Extending now to you and me
The vision of what we have done:
And as the boat drew to the quay
I thought, by crossing this short water
I shall not find, in its place,
The answer with the silent face.

p. 1950   GEORGE BARKER

From *The Sleeping Princess*

Those who travel with me
from insignificant stations
that stick in the country's throat –
cases on luggage racks,
this bucket dipped in the nation
two who play cards: one with a child: one with an axe –

carry their trades and chances
by cord or under arm
white eyes that watch a speaker
silent with one another,
privately, willing to learn
nothing, receive no news, admit no brother.

Do I carry my trade, or they
smell and distrust my verse?
If the hard crust broke, would they ask
'What have you to say?
Things are come to a pass –
the train runs on, whether we play or refuse to play.

What do you want? We sit
and wait for it. So do you.'
I look across at the hands –
four that shuffle the pack,
two are the child's, and two
holding the child, and two for the axe propped on the
    rack:

and think: look down at your own –
feel the tongue in your mouth.
My trade is shrunked down

to a negative, giving the lie
to the lie that means your death.
You in your private silence have left me the cry:

Mother is making your bed
in the Agamemnonian dark.
Your four hands shuffle your fate.
The evil axe is your own.
The papers that screen you bark
for your death, and you leave me to bellow alone

the schedule of First Aid
the procedure in case of fire.
'What can we do? Where go?
The time is out of joint –
there is nothing possible here –
our hands are single, our voice and your voice faint –

we may be healed in the end –
perhaps they are telling the truth –
we must Stand Up for our Rights –
we never have had a chance –
there is no tongue in our mouth –
the fine is forty shillings for the first offence!'

This is the work I do –
I gather your scattered No
your inarticulate salvage
of bloody-mindedness
drive your doubts in a row
as a fence between you and the eyeless, voiceless, press

of those who were Citizens
who waited another week,
whose poor disguises failed,

who did not speak soon enough,
who thought it useless to speak.
whose No was killed by custom, and they by custom
  killed.

Give me this for my work.
I ask you to speak, not hear.
I am your audience. Give
the disobedient word
that will open history's ear
like the prince's kiss that woke, and the sleepers stirred.

p. 1950   ALEX COMFORT

Index of Authors

Index of Titles

Index of First Lines

FOR THE BEST IN PAPERBACKS, LOOK FOR THE

In every corner of the world, on every subject under the sun, Penguin represents quality and variety – the very best in publishing today.

For complete information about books available from Penguin – including Pelicans, Puffins, Peregrines and Penguin Classics – and how to order them, write to us at the appropriate address below. Please note that for copyright reasons the selection of books varies from country to country.

In the United Kingdom: For a complete list of books available from Penguin in the U.K., please write to *Dept E.P. Penguin Books Ltd, Harmondsworth, Middlesex, UB7 0DA*

In the United States: For a complete list of books available from Penguin in the U.S., please write to *Dept BA, Penguin, 299 Murray Hill Parkway, East Rutherford, New Jersey 07073*

In Canada: For a complete list of books available from Penguin in Canada, please write to *Penguin Books Canada Ltd, 2801 John Street, Markham, Ontario L3R 1B4*

In Australia: For a complete list of books available from Penguin in Australia, please write to the *Marketing Department, Penguin Books Australia Ltd, P.O. Box 257, Ringwood, Victoria 3134*

In New Zealand: For a complete list of books available from Penguin in New Zealand, please write to the *Marketing Department, Penguin Books (NZ) Ltd, Private Bag, Takapuna, Auckland 9*

In India: For a complete list of books available from Penguin in India, please write to *Penguin Overseas Ltd, 706 Eros Apartments, 56 Nehru Place, New Delhi, 110019*

In Holland: For a complete list of books available from Penguin in Holland, please write to *Penguin Books Nederland B.V. Postbus 195, NL – 1380 AD WEESP Netherlands*

In Germany: For a complete list of books available from Penguin in Germany, please write to *Penguin Books Ltd, Friedrichstrasse, 10 – 12, D 6000, Frankfurt a m, Main 1, Federal Republic of Germany*

In Spain: For a complete list of books available from Penguin in Spain, please write to *Longman Penguin España, Calle San Nicolas 15, E – 28013 Madrid, Spain*

FOR THE BEST IN PAPERBACKS, LOOK FOR THE

PENGUIN BOOKS OF POETRY

American Verse
Ballads
British Poetry Since 1945
Caribbean Verse
A Choice of Comic and Curious Verse
Contemporary American Poetry
Contemporary British Poetry
Eighteenth-Century Verse
Elizabethan Verse
English Poetry 1918–60
English Romantic Verse
English Verse
First World War Poetry
Georgian Poetry
Irish Verse
Light Verse
London in Verse
Love Poetry
The Metaphysical Poets
Modern African Poetry
Modern Arab Poetry
New Poetry
Poems of Science
Poetry of the Thirties
Post-War Russian Poetry
Spanish Civil War Verse
Unrespectable Verse
Victorian Verse
Women Poets